Mayhem to Miracles

Other Books in the Sacred Stories of Transformation Series

Chaos to Clarity: Sacred Stories of Transformational Change
Crappy to Happy: Sacred Stories of Transformational Joy

Other Books by Rev. Ariel Patricia

God is in the Little Things: Messages from the Animals
God is in the Little Things: Messages from the Golden Angels
Scanning for Signal (Co-Author)

Other Books by Kathleen O'Keefe-Kanavos

Dreams That Can Save Your Life: Early Warning Signs of Cancer and Other Diseases, Kathleen O'Keefe-Kanavos (Author), Larry Burk M.D. C.E.H.P. (Author)
Surviving Cancerland: Intuitive Aspects of Healing

Sacred Stories of Transformational Hope

Mayhem
to
Miracles

True Stories of Courage, Triumph, and Peace

Rev. Ariel Patricia & Kathleen O'Keefe-Kanavos

SACRED STORIES
PUBLISHING

Mayhem to Miracles: Sacred Stories of Transformational Hope
Rev. Ariel Patricia and Kathleen O'Keefe-Kanavos

Tradepaper ISBN: 978-1-945026-78-2
Electronic ISBN: 978-1-945026-79-9

Library of Congress Control Number: 2021940116

Published by Sacred Stories Publishing, Fort Lauderdale, FL USA

The power of story
written, spoken, and lived,
allows us to deepen into the Mystery of our souls.

TABLE OF CONTENTS

ACKNOWLEDGMENTS

This third book in the *Sacred Stories of Transformation* series has been a collaborative work on many levels. I wish to thank Rev. Ariel of Sacred Stories Publishing, a co-author of all three books, for her constant inspiration and desire to continue making the Sacred Stories series a success. Through all the challenges and joys, this literary pursuit has been a profound growth experience.

A special *thank you* to all our authors, many of whom have been with us since the publication of the first book *Chaos to Clarity: Sacred Stories of Transformational Change*. Three years of working together have made them our family. Your stories written from the heart have brought *Mayhem to Miracles* to life.

To Peter, my devoted husband of almost forty years, all I can say is thank you for being my Li'l Abner in *The Face on The Pillow* story in this book and for your endless support and guidance during the labor pains and birthing of all the books. I love you.

-Kathleen O'Keefe-Kanavos

Thank you to my co-author, Kat Kanavos, for birthing the miracle of this book series with me. Through the chaos, crappy, and mayhem and into the clarity, happy, and miracles… Kat, we did it!

Deep gratitude for the miracle of our incredible contributing authors. Your courage, tenacity, and profound commitment to get through the mayhem and into the miracles is inspiring.

And to our readers: If you are in mayhem… keep going. Know that you are strong, you matter, and your beacon of hope is going to shine… look for it. We are cheering for you.

-Rev. Ariel Patricia

FOREWORD

From Never to Always
by Rev. Dr. Temple Hayes

Don't ever give up on your hopes and dreams, for you, too, can move from never to always.

I feel that I have lived many lifetimes within one. What I know for sure is that our dreams are always waiting for us to let them come true, and the things we hope and wish for in our hearts would not be there if they also were not meant to be realized. As a Spiritual Leader for thirty years, I have witnessed many miracles and dreams that people have put away and locked deep inside their consciousness.

Our dreams do not let us down; we let them down when we give up on them before they have an opportunity to come to light. I have learned that not every dream happens chronologically or by chapter in the way we feel it is supposed to.

Miracles happen when your mind is awake, and your heart is open.

Within the pages of *Mayhem to Miracles*, you will not only be introduced to new dreams and hopes, but you will also discover the greatest aspects of your heart that have been lying dormant. You will unravel the greatest miracles of all…

Me, Temple Hayes, a mom? No way could that be possible.

I spent so much time of my early adult life either recovering from alcoholic binges or moving back and forth from denial to acceptance that I was gay. It didn't even occur to me in the late '70s and '80s that having a child would be an option. I had drawn so much attention to myself during those fifteen years of rebelling and wallowing in my own *woundology*. How could I possibly be capable of managing the raising of a child when I couldn't even focus on raising me?

In the early days of sobriety, I explored a relationship with a beautiful man for five years. Although we found moments of being happy, I never fully expressed a life of indwelling happiness. He also was very clear with me that he had two adult children and wouldn't want anymore.

Despite my hope, it seemed so evident that my path was not destined to include a child.

So, I learned, as a self-helper and thought leader, to say that I chose to put my birthing energy into my career and projects. I chose to be a Spiritual Leader rather than choosing to have children.

I traveled a lot, both in the United States and internationally, but it was for the love of children that I was always drawn back into a spiritual community. I missed the joy of kids.

Every now and then, I would go on a spirit-journey with my Shaman teacher close by, and in the vision dream-state, I would hear a voice that said, "The baby is fine." Of course, I would transform the statement in my own mind to mean my visions were gestating, and all would be well. I never entertained, from an emotional place, what it would be like having a child—for as I previously declared, that ship had sailed.

In my mid-fifties, my wife, who had two adult sons, and I would, on a rare occasion, say, "We never got our little girl." A medium or psychic would tell us that a little girl would be coming into our lives, and we would talk about fostering. I would simply laugh. I have the greatest respect for people who foster anything, for I am not that person.

Once an animal or person is in my heart, there is no letting go.

As my life fast-tracked to fifty-nine prosperous years, I had just completed a Sunday service. It was a beautiful Sunday morning, and I went out into the lobby to discover a little girl with a big red bow in her hair, white tights, and shiny, black patent leather shoes. She looked at me with such intention, and I was immediately spellbound when our eyes met. I asked the lady who was with her, "Who is this bundle of a miracle?" and she said, "That's her name! Her name is Miracle." I felt the moment deeply in my heart, as the word *miracle* has always been one of my favorite words.

Each Sunday was as magical as the next. This little girl, Miracle, kept finding me in the lobby. I learned the woman with her was her grandmother and her soon-to-be mom.

Miracle was just turning two, and every time she saw me, she would cry to connect with me. I realized one Sunday just how drawn she was to me when she couldn't find me and I heard her crying. When I opened the door, she gasped as if holding her breath and said my name, as best she could, over and over again.

She would always gasp when she found me at our center. To clarify, we are on a two-and-a-half-acre lot. She would often have to search for a while until we were together again. Eventually, she learned to say two words which she says to this day: "Hold me, hold me, hold me."

During the beginning of our connection, I told her grandmother I would join her in court, because she was adopting Miracle as her daughter. What a beautiful time we shared. They gifted me with a drum for helping them. That summer, unbeknownst to me, my shaman teacher had died. It had made me sad that she did not bequeath me her drum.

The drum Miracle gave me was almost identical to the one Berenice had owned, so I knew my shaman friend was involved from the spirit world. I also discovered, from a reputable astrologist, that Miracle was born the same day that my chart said I would have a child.

This new reality was chipping away at my heart, as I was beginning to profoundly see that a miracle was in the making. One day in my office, I learned that one of my close friends had died. I had said goodbye to three close friends, all within a few weeks.

I was wailing from these deaths as I settled into my office chair and let all my feelings emerge. Simultaneously, at another location, Miracle said to her mom, "My Momma Temple needs a hug. Mom, you need to give her a hug. She's crying, she's crying…" Miracle was three. Her mom texted me and said, "What is going on? Miracle is beside herself."

When she was just learning to say her words, she would interrupt me after Sunday service when I was talking with someone and get in the middle of us to say, "This is my Temple, my Temple."

We had to prepare her for when I would go out of town, and when I wasn't at the community, she didn't want to go. When I would be in Europe, she would automatically adjust to my time zone without any discussions to guide her.

She had chosen me, and to me, it was likened to Eastern teachings when the child picks their teacher. Our love and connection were filled with wonder and miracles.

In the first year or so of our relationship, I felt sorry for her "Grandmother-mom" because Miracle never wanted to leave my house. As endearing as it was, I knew it wasn't easy for her mom to understand. Over time, I worked with Miracle and her fears. I realized her room had energies, which she felt deeply, as a sensitive child.

I encouraged her mom to go through every item in Miracle's room and let her decide what she would keep or release. She used her intuition and her sensitivities to create an entirely different space in her life. Miracle, at three-and-a-half years old, had now created the energy of the room she wanted, and she was never afraid again.

I have witnessed the most extraordinary times in my life these past three years as Miracle has opened my heart to so much magic and many new possibilities.

I am now Miracle's legal guardian. She spends half her time each week at my house.

She is my little girl, and I am her Momma Temple. I went from never having a child to always being a mom.

There's a refrigerator magnet that says, "The best is yet to come. If it hasn't, it isn't over yet."

Having a daughter has been one of my greatest miracles.

Don't ever give up on your hopes and dreams, for you, too, can move from never to always.

The Spirituality of Hope
by Rev. Ariel Patricia

Hope is not a four-letter word.

Some people in spiritual circles will tell you that *hope* is a four-letter word of the worst kind. To be hopeful or to hope for something, they say, means that you are not spiritual—because saying the word "hope" implies you don't have a deep enough faith or knowing in a Universe that supports you.

What drivel!

They will also tell you that you are here to learn lessons, and if you don't learn your lesson, it will keep repeating itself—or worse yet, you will keep creating situations for the lesson to be learned.

Seriously?

So, we are here to go through some *sh*t*... I think for our own good(?)... but we can't be hopeful as we slog through the deep mud of the blooming lotus flower. We just have to know that everything is working out for our highest and best?

Can we make up any sillier or more difficult rules?

What a conundrum we have created for ourselves! As if there isn't enough mayhem in this world already. Where is the journey? How can we be the heroes and heroines of our stories, riding off into the sunset with the music playing and the credits rolling, if we didn't overcome something?

Half kidding aside, I do believe that getting to a place of deep knowing is the spiritual seeker's journey. In our book *Crappy to Happy: Sacred Stories of Transformational Joy*, I discuss this and share that knowing is the peace in which joy resides.

But you have to get there first.

Years ago, I wrote:

And then sometimes
There is only me.
Relief and loneliness at the same time.
There is a beauty to the certainty.

That is the part of the journey where *hope* is necessary.

In this book, I share two stories of when I was deep in the mud of the lotus. I was down so deep that my beautiful flower had not yet broken through the mud to see the golden light of the sun. You will read similar stories from kindred souls, and perhaps you may have a similar story or two yourself. It's okay. You are experiencing life. All of it. The high fives and the down lows. And you're not alone.

In these same stories, you will see the blazing beacon of hope shining through. Look for it. Cheer for it. Hope is our guiding light, friendly face, and welcoming hand. Hope is not a four-letter word. Hope is our journey through to the miracle.

Feeling hopeful,

Ariel

The Psychology of Hope
by Kathleen O'Keefe-Kanavos

*The collective search for hope is so huge, so all-pervasive,
yet few even recognize how profound it is. The thread of hope
weaved during crisis connects our Universal
Oneness to Quantum Entanglement.*

In the previous book, *Crappy to Happy*, which focused on joy, James Redfield (who wrote *The Celestine Prophecy*) described the book's message as *The Art of the Comeback*. *Mayhem to Miracles* is all about hope, which like miracles, comes in many forms. What is the psychology behind our obsession with hope, and what exactly is hope? I believe hope is The Art of Resilience.

Mayhem to Miracles is the natural progression of the Sacred Story three-book series about transformation. The first book, *Chaos to Clarity*, focused on change for a better life. In the second book, *Crappy to Happy*, joy was the result of change; and finally, *Mayhem to Miracles* builds on both change and joy to spotlight hope, which goes a step beyond a better life to a better future. Change-Joy-Hope.

Today's world is filled with mayhem that is not the result of one specific or chaotic event, like our emotional disconnection from each other, from ourselves, from nature, and from family. It is the consistent, day-in-day-out trauma of living in a world often felt to be disconnected from hope, and seemingly blind to its miracles. Currently, there is a collective cry for hope—hope for a future beyond COVID, lockdowns, failed businesses, and disconnected relationships.

Despite all we have experienced, that glimmer of hope is still alive.

What is hope, and what is the Psychology behind its triumph over despair? We desperately seek it as part of the human race and Universal Oneness.

Hope is the glue that binds us individually and as a collective unit to keep us resilient.

Mayhem to Miracles carries on the time-honored tradition of storytelling by weaving unique, life-changing, and hope-inspired stories into a book filled with personal interactions felt worldwide. We decided to create a book filled with this illusive thing called hope because this collective search for hope is so huge, so all-pervasive, yet few even recognize how profound it is. Hope is enlightening and lifesaving, as seen in the story by Rev. Sandra Kitt.

Enlightenment is the antidote to individual despair and collective despair. Our spiritual journey is not limited to the path of the individual because we're challenged as nations, and ultimately as a species, to become the embodiment of our more triumphant and loving selves.

Hope can change the course of illness, the future, love, and lives.

Since the time of ancient Greece, human beings have believed that hope is essential to life. In Greek mythology, Elpis (Ancient Greek: ἐλπίς) is described as the spirit of hope which is the antidote to despair.[1] The search for hope is most urgent during times of mayhem. *Mayhem to Miracles* brings us into the lives of people at pivotal moments when they find hope—or moments when it eludes their grasp. Through these intimate portraits, we learn why some people feel undeserving of it until hope finds them.

If the psychology of hope is mental and physical resilience, can hope contribute to recovery by changing our physical well-being? The second part of the book, titled *Health And Well-Being: I'll Stand By You,* is full of stories that say, "Yes!" To delve more into this hotly debated question, I researched cutting-edge information for researchers who unraveled what they labeled as the *biology of hope.* Is there a scientific basis for understanding the role of this strong emotion in the outcome of illness?

Science and psychology are thinking about hope in new ways. According to research published by Jerome Groopman, "We are just beginning to appreciate hope's reach. I see hope as the very heart of healing."[2]

Perhaps hope's limits are undefined and statistically unmeasurable because hope is limitless.

Although there is no uniform definition of hope, it is often felt to be the elevated feeling we believe is the path to a better future. The power of hope prevails despite, or in deference to, the significant obstacles, mayhem, and deep pitfalls met along the path to our future.

True hope embraces miracles. Hope is medicine when all else fails. It gives us the courage to confront our circumstances and gives us the emotional fortitude to overcome them.

Our lives are complicated puzzles with pieces strewn about the hallways of our minds. Hope helps us put our pieces together.

As a teacher of special needs children in the public school system and a professor of psychology, the shattered pieces of lives and personal experience often opened my eyes to the darkness of despair in my student's eyes. My job was to replace the darkness with the burning light of hope. Hope could not be measured but could be seen and felt by the individual and those around them. It is the fertile ground in which miracles grow and are fed by faith. It pushes us to take chances and not give up or give in to despair.

Mind over matter is the psychology of hope creating the biology of hope; someone's belief can create a physical result. Researchers are learning that change in mindset has the power to alter neurochemistry.

The key elements of hope are belief and expectation. They can block pain by releasing the brain's endorphins and encephalin, which mimics the effects of morphine. The psychological impact of hope can have a significant effect on physiological processes like respiration, circulation, and motor functions. Teresa Velardi's story exemplifies how a belief in an afterlife helps with the crippling neurological and physical pain when dying. The hope of seeing loved ones "one last time" and the joy of connecting with family in the afterlife can transform death's pain into relief during the last hours of life.

Hope can start a chain reaction during illness that makes improvement and healing more likely, exemplified by Diane Vich's story.

Each story in the book embraces the hope that housed a miracle.

Mayhem to Miracles takes us to the hidden places of our imagination, memory, and reality. These stories can touch something deep within us—something that goes beyond mere facts and cold, calculated logic to empower us with transformational insights. We're left hopeful during times of worldwide transformation. The stories tucked into this book's pages give examples of the power of hope in the face of uncertainty within family backgrounds, experiences in the workplace, travel, personal habits, relationships, and faith. Authors share tales of adventure, intrigue, love, and hope.

These fantastic stories are about real people, like you and me. The footprints they leave on the pathways of our minds can be a sense of support and guidance in our lives, often in ways that may astound us. There are no little people, small places, victims, unimportant events, or insignificant encounters in these stories.

The thread of hope weaved during crisis connects our Universal Oneness to Quantum Entanglement.

I hope some of these stories ignite your imagination, while the message of hope in others might catch you by surprise as you discover amazing new things about yourself and the people you thought you knew. Most of all, I hope the stories will inspire you to discover and tell your own story of mayhem to miracles.

PART 1

LOVE AND RELATIONSHIPS
Crazy Little Thing Called Love

I want to break open with emotion,
for love to permeate every fiber of my being.

The Face on the Pillow
by Kathleen O'Keefe-Kanavos

My dreams came true when the Face on the Pillow
became the love of my life.

My three eight-year-old best friends and I sit on the ornate living room rug and play with our Barbie dolls as American armored tanks roll down the street to face Russian tanks lining up along the east side of the Berlin Wall. Our mothers whisper words of hopeful reassurance to each other as they sit around the dining room table and watch us play. For our sake, they hide their fear while facing the uncertain winds of war.

As we play, a mother whispered, "Do you think we'll still be alive tomorrow?"
"Shhh!" came the reply. "The children…"

It was 1961, and the Berlin Wall had gone up last night. When our telephone rang at three a.m., my father said, "Red Alert. You and Kathy will be evacuated later today. No suitcases. Stay with the other wives and wait for word." We were officially in a war zone.

1

Now, as my best friends and I played and waited to be airlifted out of harm's way, the conversation shifted to our uncertain future.

"You know, I think Kathy will be the first one of the girls to get married," Donna's mother said, rubbing her swollen legs. She was pregnant again.

"Really? Why is that?" my mother asked.

"Because she's the prettiest and the most popular."

"Kathy, are you going to get married first?" Mom jokingly asked.

"No! I won't get married until I'm twenty-six or twenty-seven," I answered, pulling my Barbie's dress off over her head.

The mothers all rocked with laughter.

"And I'll bet you are going to marry a prince because you are such a little princess—right, Kathy?" Deana's mom asked. Her strong German accent made my name sound like Cat-y.

"No. I am going to marry a millionaire," I said, pulling some psychedelic-print bell-bottom pants on Barbie.

Everyone laughed except my mom. "How do you know that?" she asked.

"Because I've seen him," I replied, making Barbie dance in her new pants.

Everyone stopped laughing and stared at me. The look on my mom's face screamed *Pedophile*! "Kathy, where and when have you seen him?" she asked.

"On my pillow at night, in my dreams. It's always the same face on the pillow looking at me. He's really handsome and has big brown eyes…"

A sigh of relief escaped from all the mothers' mouths. No madman was on the playground trying to steal a child. "Oh, thank goodness, it's just Kathy's dreams again," Diane's mom said.

My dream was quickly dismissed as a childhood fantasy as the whispered conversation returned to the clear and present danger.

Eighteen years later, after a broken engagement, sitting in my car at a red light in Fort Myers, Florida, quite sure I would never find the right person to spend the rest of my life with, I decided to have a little chat with God.

"Look," I said to God, "I just had to gently reject another questionable date for the weekend. Do you really expect me not to step over these men you are putting in my way? Seriously, if there is someone you want me to be with for the rest of my life, please bring him on. If I am to stay single for the rest of my life, that is fine, too—but please don't send me any more losers or weirdos to reject. I'm almost twenty-six years old and don't have time for this anymore. What must I do to find the true love of my life?"

A week later, a fellow teacher was having second thoughts about her impending divorce and asked me to meet her for a chat in the local hotel bar that passed as a club on the weekends. She felt I might understand her emotions, since I had broken off a five-year engagement before moving to Florida. Although I avoided bars, her desperate need to talk overpowered my disdain for the place. I agreed to meet.

At the club's door, all the women were given bolts as party-favors while the men were handed screws. *What strange and cheap party favors*, I thought as I nonchalantly tossed mine on the table.

"I've been with him since high school… even followed him to Vietnam and lived close to his base during his tour, but… that feeling is gone. And I wonder if it was ever really right," my friend said. "I never followed my dreams, just him. I've always had a different kind of man in mind for a husband. One who would encourage me, not compete with me. Do you know what I mean?" She wrapped both hands around her drink as if they were someone's neck.

"Yes. I do know what you mean. We all have our 'Dream Lover,'" I replied. My mind reflected on my earlier conversation with God.

It soon became apparent that attempting to have a private conversation in the club was almost impossible.

The chairs around our table quickly became filled with men who offered us drinks, dances, and their screws. Yes, their screws!

We did not realize at the time that the first Saturday every November (since 1938) was Sadie Hawkins Day.

Cartoonist Al Capp invented Sadie Hawkins Day in his Li'l Abner comic strip. As a child, my mom read the Sunday morning "funny papers" to me, and one of my favorite cartoons was Li'l Abner. My being at the party was synchronicity on so many levels.

The story behind the party was that Sadie Hawkins—the homely, unwed daughter of the Mayor of hillbilly Dog Patch—pursued the top eligible bachelors in a run-for-your-life foot race. The ultimate prize was matrimony, often at gunpoint, for Sadie and any other spinsters who were able to "chase down their catch."

And here I am, a Sadie Hawkins… at the ultimate spinster party. OMG!

But the goal at this party is not to run men down but rather to find your perfect screw. I threw my bolt on the floor and kicked it away after a Neanderthal's almost fit.

Just when I couldn't take anymore and prepared to leave, in walked the Face on the Pillow. Even in the dark light, it was an exact match.

The Face confidently walked up and asked me to dance. It was instant karma.

Power and confidence are attractive to me. This gorgeous Greek with sun-streaked hair instantly drew me into his eyes. They were the most beautiful soft brown eyes I'd ever seen. I fell in love with Peter's eyes, the windows to his soul, the eyes I'd seen on my pillow when I was eight years old.

We spent the next three years together until the day his parents, my in-laws, gave us a society wedding at Copley Plaza in Boston. My father-in-law always joked, "Kathy ran from Peter just fast enough to catch him." He was right. I got my Li'l Abner.

If Peter was my Li'l Abner, then I was his Daisy Mae.

With Peter by my side, I felt God had answered my prayers. "Ask, and ye shall receive," had worked. God always hears. We've been together for more than forty years, through thick and thin, for better or worse. Even throughout my breast cancer and recurrence, which came under "'till death do you part." My dreams came true when the Face on the Pillow became the love of my life.

My Son and Me
by Laura Staley

Two lives, like two pearls formed from all that grit inside the oyster.

On a bright, sun-shining, crisp autumn day, text messages from my son's dad and his sister ping my phone. "He sent a message to me saying he loved me, telling me goodbye. You must find him right now!"

I run out the door of my office onto the flat roof over the garage. I spot the ladder that he used to climb to the highest rooftop of the house. I scream his name. He charges over toward the ladder, roaring with rage, grabs hold, and hurls it into the backyard. I hear it clatter and crash to the ground. My heart pounds. I dial 911. I feel my body center itself. I breathe deeply.

I become the eye of the storm.

Within moments I hear the wailing sirens of several emergency vehicles. The flashing red lights reflect in my periphery vision as my eyes remain glued to my son: his shoulders hunched in his red jacket, a knit hat on top of his head, body crouched on the edge of the roof, a knapsack close to his body.

I hear the officers at the front door. I walk quickly back inside the house and down the stairs to let them in and guide them to the location of my son. I call his dad. He answers, "I really cannot talk right now. We're on our way to dinner with my parents."

I hang up. He's in Florida with family.

I stay focused on my son, who now has cops on either side of him, holding his arms. He yells and writhes. "Let me go!"

My best friend appears, seemingly out of nowhere. With an arm around my shoulders, she gently guides me back into the house.

"You don't need to see this, sweetheart. You've seen enough." She and I walk downstairs together.

My daughter bursts into the house. We hug each other. She's crying. I remain centered.

"Does my dad not think this is actually happening? He keeps telling me he can't talk right now! Oh my God, Mom!"

I hold her as she sobs. She had chosen this weekend to return home in the midst of her first semester of college.

Her move-in day had already been wrecked by the proverbial straw that broke the back of her parents' marriage: the ugly truths that came to light before I drove her to college that day. My son's daily contact with both his sister and dad ended on that day.

Internally—on that God-awful, broken-open day—I anchored to a vision: "Single, Happy, Free Laura Staley." This declaration became my empowering, guiding light.

"Laura, he's in an ambulance headed to the emergency room. We need to get to the hospital."

Later, I learned my son had broken free from the police officers and had dashed toward the bridge over a rushing river, two blocks from our house. The officers had apprehended him before he got there. His breaking free and running made sense. He's a natural athlete, a cross-country and track runner, and an excellent student who tested gifted and talented in many subjects. And he's a sensitive, troubled teen.

My son is admitted to a psychiatric facility.

A plan was created for structures to be in place for ongoing support upon his release. I felt determined, over-whelmed, and grateful for the trauma-release work I had invested in for more than a decade. I knew how to keep returning to my core: a cracking, burning fire desire for freedom that had been stoked for at least a decade. I connected to the optimistic, fierce fighter embedded in my soul.

I was the primary caregiver of my teen son. Though he had firmly stated he wanted to split time between his dad and me, which I completely supported, his dad's living situation did not accommodate.

The months that followed involved responding to life's constant challenges and taking brave new actions. Some of these included my daughter's parked vehicle damaged, a window shattered by a hit and run, a washing machine breaking, both dogs becoming ill or injured, then one dog dying, and two dear friends dying.

I researched survival jobs, attended business networking events, and hired a new attorney. I answered emails and filled out papers, paid bills, and met with my attorney. I met with my realtor and hired contractors to prepare the house for sale. I cleaned gutters, shoveled snow, cleaned the house, cleared clutter, and sold the house. I visited my daughter and moved her back home after spring semester in time to move to a new house. And I showed up at the courthouse with my attorney each time with a cherished friend by my side.

Riding a surfboard through crashing ocean waves as the life I knew fell apart, I became a midwife for my new life. I monitored my son's life and his school activities, his comings and goings. I drove him to his therapists' offices regularly.

I vividly remember one evening after completing an interview, I got in my vehicle, my entire body shaking, and searched the neighborhood, looking for my despondent son. He had left the house on a dark, cold, winter night. I found him when he finally returned my phone call.

Choking on tears, I emphatically said, "I *love* you! I won't *ever* stop loving you!"

I worried constantly about my son. I met with therapists, the school counselor, and the principal and attempted open-hearted conversations with him as best as I could. I knew the essence of his character, his heart-centered qualities, and his previous challenges.

In pre-school, my son played with every child.

He interacted with the children with whom no other children played. One teacher described him as the "classroom social worker." He made great friends—yet, at times, he expressed a loneliness I struggled to fully understand. He exuded humor, warmth, likeability, conscientiousness, empathy, and an emotional awareness that most adults struggle to cultivate.

During elementary school, he told me about the adults who acted kind with other adults and then became very angry and mean toward children. His dad, he, and I met with his elementary school art teacher. My son bravely told him he felt scared in his classroom because the art teacher yelled angrily at children and threw away certain children's artwork when they didn't help with clean-up. The art teacher turned red-faced and fiercely defended his deeds and attitude. He declared he had been teaching for thirty years and that he had no issue with my compliant boy. The art teacher dismissed my son's fears.

At nine years old, my son also felt the pain of the discord of his parents' marriage.

"Will you and dad stop arguing?"

I was in couple's therapy with my then-husband at this juncture. I offered, "Your dad and I are smart people. We're working with a therapist. We'll figure this out."

"But what if you don't?"

His question lingered in the air, unanswered.

I remember how painful my silence had felt.

I faced each day now living the answer to that fateful question. I wept, barely slept, adapted, pivoted constantly, broke wide open, screamed alone in my car, shook with terror, and lost weight I didn't need to lose. I became fierce, emboldened, strong, confident, and capable. A hundred FFTs (F*cking First Times) fueled me. Daily runs or bicycle rides, yoga practice, and meditation became non-negotiable necessities to my physical strength, emotional acuity, and mental flexibility during these many dark months of my soul.

The fury I felt toward my ex-husband fired passionate actions for my emancipation and fierce commitment to my son's well-being. Yet, as I grew stronger inside all the fresh, courageous actions I took, my son's life became more unstable, dark, and unpredictable.

While I knew I was powerless in the face of my son's many dangerous choices—some I knew about and some I learned about much later—I also experienced this unwavering optimism deep inside for him. I discovered deeper layers of unconditional love, even as the external realities continued to roar. Internally, I declared his thriving life, which in some ways resembled the one I held for myself.

I trusted his growth, his character qualities, and I knew the healing of his mental and emotional challenges was possible. I believed in him and the quality of his life as fervently as I had begun to believe in my own. I also knew his brain had not yet fully developed. He'd become immersed in treacherous waters, and I found myself showing up for him while simultaneously paddling my own life to solid ground.

In late summer his dad moved. My son began living with his dad for a week and returning to my house for the next week, in accordance with the decree.

When school resumed, my son's behavior became more erratic, his emotions volatile. During the week of homecoming, he broke the house rules I'd firmly established with him. I grounded him and took his cell phone for a week. He was furious. He let me know there were no consequences at his dad's house. After another difficult interaction with my son about his choices and behavior, he left my house to live full time with his dad.

I continued to receive calls from the school counselor about my son's outbursts and disrespectful behaviors. I then learned from the counselor that he had received an unusual leave of absence for medical reasons, which his dad had requested. While I had been in constant, fact-based communication with his dad every step of the way, his dad fell silent with me during this time. I became even more anxious, even as I nurtured the vision, the unconditional love.

12

A week before Christmas, I received an email from my son's dad saying he would be traveling out of state for the upcoming weekend. I sent a fiery email. I received no reply.

The epic party happened at his dad's house.

My son was rushed to the ER. Within forty-eight hours, I walked a long, hot, stuffy basement hallway with an orderly and my subdued son in a wheelchair to the same psychiatric facility he had been admitted to fourteen months earlier.

My focus shifted fully to the life of my son. Working with a compassionate healthcare mentor, I found an excellent program out of state. His dad, once he experienced firsthand the imploded state of my son, agreed to have him placed there. Three days after Christmas, he was escorted from the hospital to an out-of-state program.

My son engaged in meaningful work in this program. He awakened to the fact that he had done "f-ed up things, but that he wasn't a f-up." As part of his internal work, he wrote letters to both his dad and I accounting for every single thing he remembered doing and saying, coming clean with his actual life and experiences.

I read that letter thoroughly and experienced much heartache and shock as he poured out every dark truth. Facing his resentments and his past actions affirmed that I could continue to do the same in my life. Looking at myself fully in the mirror; owning imperfections, angry words spoken, unresolved traumas, and unhealthy patterns of behavior; recognizing selfishness and unworthiness; and then choosing new thoughts and behaviors remain courageous work that composts the soil for healing, for new life.

My son chose to be placed in a longer-term facility in a different state.

A few months later, I opened a handwritten letter. I wept as I read his heartfelt words.

Dear Mom, Man, it's been a long ride. Seventeen years of ups and downs in our relationship and we both had our separate struggles. However, something that has been consistent throughout these years is you have showed up for me. You've been there when I was a young kid in preschool and I decided to grow out my bangs; then I really got sick and tired of not being able to see, so I chopped them off. And you were there: I remember you telling me, "It's your life, it's your hair." You were there for me in third grade when I was getting bullied, to pull me out of that situation and take matters into your own hands. You attempted to teach me even though you have no experience as an elementary school teacher, and you supported me in finding the best program for me to finish elementary school. On the other hand, you were there for me when I was at my worst even though there must have been so many emotions rushing through you, you were there to support me and take the best action to save my life. When I was at my worst depressed states in my life, there you were expending everything in your power to support me and expecting nothing in return. For being able to show up for me every day and when I couldn't do it for myself, I am forever so grateful. There are really no words to describe how grateful I am for the love and support you have shown me.

He got jobs while finishing his high school classes and earned enough money to purchase a car. My daughter and I cheered for him when he graduated from the program, and again while watching his high school graduation ceremony. He landed a good, full-time job and moved to an apartment.

He shared more amends with me in person, as tears streamed down my face. "You did what any loving mom would do. My past actions and words were mine, Mom."

Now five years sober, my son currently works with young men in recovery. His life completely transformed from the inside out, and so did mine. I relocated to the mountains of North Carolina, to create dance videos to inspire contributions to people's lives. I write personal essays and work over Zoom with clients. I fell in love with the joy of being alive.

Two lives, like two pearls formed from all that grit inside the oyster. Together, we reflect the essence of each other's souls and character qualities. My son and I turned from being mirrors for each other toward shining our bright, radiant lights in love and service to people awakening in the world.

From knowing the experience of believing in and loving my son, I learned to deeply believe in and unconditionally love myself.

Mary Queen
by Lori Walker

Her kindness connected us and she will always be a part of me.

ome people get it right the first time. They meet the love of their life while they are young, get married, have kids, and the white picket fence is always freshly painted. And then there is me.

Being the youngest of five children had its ups and downs. I watched my brothers and sisters intently, always wondering what it would be like to bigger and stronger than them. I felt like I was always the last in line, the one who was left behind. As a teenager, I would dream of running away to travel the world.

I couldn't ask for a better plan than the one that unfolded.

My high school boyfriend joined the Army and was stationed at Fort Stewart, Georgia. Thrilled, I boarded a plane and joined him. New places, new friends, and a new beginning. My dream was coming true!

But ever so slowly, reality crept in. The drudgery of daily life, having very little money, and homesickness started taking their toll. We grew apart, and he had an affair. One night, he forgot to pick me up from work. When he finally staggered in, we had a huge argument. Because he wasn't winning, he decided the best thing to do was to hit me. The blow landed on the side of my head, and a lump started to form. I'll never forget the look of sheer regret on his face. But it was too late. I could never trust him again. A few days later, I was gone.

I should have returned home to Pittsburgh, but I wasn't ready. I moved in with my friend, Tammy, from work, and we enjoyed going out to the local clubs. Our favorite was the EM (Enlisted Men's) Club. Tammy had a crush on a guy named Mike. One night as we were sitting at our usual table, Mike and his friend came over. Mike's friend smiled at me and later, he told me that he had been watching me for weeks. He knew I was The One. The beginning of the relationship was absolute bliss.

I had only known him for two months when he received his orders for Kuwait. It was the beginning of Desert Shield. Initially, his unit was positioned so that they wouldn't see combat. But plans changed, and the eighteen-year-old kid that I had met came home a very different man. One significant consequence of his Post Traumatic Stress Disorder would alter the course of our lives.

Sex addiction is a hard thing to talk about.

There is guilt and shame on both sides. You both make excuses, apologize, and say it's going to get better. But without the right psychiatric treatment, it's hopeless. At first, it was phone sex. Later, there were actual affairs. We blamed the PTSD, and I vowed to be there for him. I was going to be his rock. I would save this man from his pain. I was The One he loved.

We married in 1991, and I became pregnant with my son a year later. In 1993, his enlistment was ending. If he reenlisted, he would be sent to Korea. We decided to move to Boise, Idaho to be near his mother. I was never told if he continued to use phone sex, but my mother-in-law did let us know that she was discontinuing her long-distance phone service.

Since neither of us had college educations, work was extremely difficult to find. And with a baby, child-care was also a dilemma. He decided to go back into the Army and was sent to Oklahoma for another round of basic training. I went back to Pittsburgh to await our next assignment. He struggled, and within four months, he was discharged because of his PTSD.

Financially, we were a mess. We worked opposite shifts so someone would always be there with John. He worked day shift for a security company, and I worked second shift at a convenience store. After a few years, he was hired by the Department of Corrections. I was promoted several times, eventually becoming the store manager. After my promotion, I switched to days, and he worked nights.

We barely saw each other, and when we were together, it was hell. By this time, his verbal abuse was intolerable. Nothing was ever good enough. I was punished with the words "you stupid bitch" daily. Imagine your preschool age son hearing his mother being treated that way. I looked forward to the days when it was quiet.

But in the quiet, things go wrong, too. He started going out after work with his friends. One night, he came home with a tattoo of an eagle on his chest. He said his friend had loaned him the money. When he was showing it off to one of our friends, our friend asked how much it had cost. He said, "Do you want to know how much I paid, or how much I told Lori?"

At first, I thought he was lying about money, but he finally admitted that his girlfriend had paid for it. *Girlfriend?* I wasn't expecting that. She would come over in the mornings when I was at work and my son was at preschool.

I forgave him for the affair.

He was very convincing when he wanted to be. I didn't want to be a 30-year-old single mother, and I was afraid my son wouldn't forgive me if I left his father. And deep down, I desperately wanted to believe things would get better. I wanted to find the man I fell in love with. I thought my devotion and forgiveness could change him. Things calmed down, and somehow seemed better for the next year. I was completely unaware that life had more drama in store.

My husband decided it was time for him to get in shape. I was proud that he lost a few pounds so quickly and thrilled that he found something that made him feel good. But his moods were changing, and I could see sadness in his eyes. One day, as I was walking out the door, he said, "I'm just not happy." My heart already knew what was coming.

My reply was simply, "Whatever you do, do it fast."

A few days after that conversation, I came home to a ransacked house. Almost everything was gone. I had no warning. I had a strong instinct there was someone else, but he wouldn't admit it at first. I told him I didn't understand why he left. I needed to make sense of it all. And finally, when he confessed these words, it shattered my heart into a million pieces.

"Yes, there is somebody else. And John has already met her. She is going to be part of my life."

A thousand questions raced through my mind. How long had this been going on? How dare you put my son in that position? Why was I never good enough? How could you break my heart again? I dropped the phone, stumbled forward, then collapsed onto the concrete floor. I was crying uncontrollably. When a horrific sob escaped my throat, I remember thinking how unnatural it sounded.

Mary Queen helped me.

A few weeks earlier, I had been looking for a reliable person for the night shift. A woman named Mary Queen had applied. One of the employees was a friend of Mary's, and she confided in me that Mary had recently lost her husband. She was having trouble sleeping, so the night shift would be a perfect fit. She was twenty years older than me, and very professional. It felt awkward at first. It seemed like we wouldn't have anything in common.

Mary entered the back room and came to my side.

"Stand up!" she said.

But I couldn't move. She pulled me to my feet and braced me against the wall. She took my face into her hands and said, "Look at me! You are going to be stronger and more beautiful than you ever imagined! Do you understand me?"

With tears streaming down my face, I asked, "Why? Why would you help me? You don't even know me!"

Her response was simple. "Because I've been there."

Thirty-three years earlier, Mary had been the victim of domestic violence and infidelity. Her abuse was far worse than mine. When she was nineteen years old, she became pregnant with her first son. Her husband moved from Pittsburgh to Washington, DC. He had family there, found work, and sent for her.

His affairs were blatant. When she tried to confront him, he would beat her. As a young mother, so far from home, she didn't know where to turn for help. One night, her husband said he was going out with some friends. She asked to go along but was told to stay home. His sisters came by the apartment looking for him. When they found Mary alone, they decided to take her with them. As fate would have it, they ended up at the same party. He was so angry that she had disobeyed him, he took her outside and slapped her until she fell to the ground. That was the final straw. She called her mother, and soon after that, she was on a flight back to Pittsburgh.

Mary would eventually find the man of her dreams, Robert Queen. I never had the chance to meet Bob, but when she spoke of him, you could both see and feel love radiate from her. I believe he treated her with the dignity and grace she deserved. She truly became The Queen. If someone told me while I was growing up that my Guardian Angel would be a beautiful Black woman, I would have never believed it. But love doesn't see color; it only sees more love.

The days, weeks, and months ahead would prove to be extremely difficult.

Dissolving a marriage is a brutal process. I had no idea of the complexity of the emotions that were about to overtake me. I was seeing a therapist who suggested I try antidepressants. I couldn't bring myself to believe that medicating was the answer. I felt everything so deeply, and I couldn't understand how a drug could make the constant thoughts go away. The depression was overwhelming.

I still had to maintain contact with my husband, because of our son. His favorite weapon was to threaten to take custody. I was scared, so I told Mary. I made a list of emergency contacts and explained that, if anything happened to me, he would be responsible.

At the same time, my grief and confusion were so unbearable, I started flirting with the idea of suicide. The emotional pain was manifesting physically. Not only did my heart hurt, but my entire body ached constantly. I just wanted all the pain to stop.

One morning, I woke up and decided it would be my last day. I wanted everything to be over. I went to work as usual, but in the back of my mind, I knew I was going to end my life that night. I had made plans with my oldest sister to watch my son for a few days. I also had a counseling appointment that night, but I had no intentions of keeping it.

The second she saw me, Mary knew.

When she asked what was wrong, I told her that he threatened me again, and I reminded her of the emergency contact list. I wanted her to know something, but I didn't want her to talk me out of my plan.

At about ten that morning, the phone calls started flooding in. My mother, both sisters, my brothers, and finally, my pastor were mysteriously checking on me. Later, I would find out that Mary called every one of them because she knew I was in serious trouble. Each conversation brought me back a little bit, but I was convinced the comfort was only temporary.

I drove my son to my sister's that afternoon. While my brother-in-law occupied John, my sister and I went to another room. She told me she knew what I was planning to do and begged me to change my mind.

She said, "I don't know what I would do without you. Please don't leave us. John needs you."

I finally heard the urgency in her voice. I watched her shaking hands pull me toward her and felt her hot tears against my cheek. The walls around my heart collapsed. She had gotten through. I promised her I would make it to my counseling session. And I did.

Who saved me on two of the darkest days of my life? My Angel, Mary Queen.

When an unhealthy relationship ends, you finally see it clearly. If you think you are alone, you're not. There is someone out there who has had a similar experience. They will light the path and show you the way. Open your heart, seek counseling, read books, take classes—and never stop learning! Sometimes, angels are just ordinary people who help you believe in miracles again.

Over the next twenty years, Mary and I would have many deep conversations. One of my questions was, "How could I ever repay you?"

Her smile and wisdom came so easily. "Someday, someone is going to need you. Pay it forward."

Mary is now dying. Cancer has ravished her body. Although I will miss her dearly, she will always be a part of me. Her kindness connected us, and our love will bind us for eternity.

I made it through the storm. Someday, I hope I can provide comfort to someone on their darkest day. Because I've been there—and someone did it for me.

From the Edge of Death to the Gift of Life
by LE Gray

I discovered the sweet gold—the light buried inside of me.

I did not tell anyone the truth, as The Monster had me convinced that no one would ever believe me. I did, however, share my secret with the numerous "friends" I created who would support me in what would become my lifelong healing process.

Cathy doesn't like many people. And she distrusts most of them. With her Marlboro smokes, spiked hair, and a fake diamond earring, she presents a tough exterior. I was about four years old when we met in the front seat of a late 1960s Ford, so I know from firsthand experience that Cathy's heart is in the right place. I know that she would fiercely protect anyone she loved.

However, she can still scare the shit out of me.

My parents are devout Roman Catholics.

They met in the eighth grade and married young. When I was born, my mother already had seven children under the age of eleven. We lived on a cul-de-sac in a four-bedroom home with one shower, one television, and one rotary telephone.

There were sixteen similar homes on Luanna Drive, with sixty school-age kids. Like so many large Catholic families, we loaded up in our wood-paneled station wagon and filed into a blonde oak pew for mass every Sunday.

To meet our family's needs and pay Catholic school tuition, my father worked two jobs. During the day, he worked in an office. At night, he sold shoes at a local store. I often waited up to hear his blue, sherbet-colored car hit the bump on our street. This meant he would soon be home to tuck me in or hoist me onto his shoulders for a walk under the stars.

In the 1960s and 1970s, it was considered an honor to host the parish priest in your home.

I called ours The Monster. He appeared to be as tall as he was wide, with a head of slick, gray hair and silver-rimmed glasses. His face was rough, like a prehistoric crater. When The Monster arrived, a snack tray with potato chips and pop was promptly placed in front of him as he settled into his favorite vinyl chair and beckoned me to "come sit on my lap."

Each time my mom entered the room, my eyes frantically sought to connect with hers with the hope that she would tell him to stop. While I bounced on those thick, dinosaur legs—his hands hurting me under my dress—my parents would ask if he needed anything. I assumed they must not have known what he was doing to me. After all, they let him stay for a delicious dinner.

Sometimes, The Monster would come over and take me for a ride to pick up milk or bread for our family. Panic-stricken at the thought of being alone with him, I would take my Raggedy Ann doll. His car, a late 1960s Ford, had one long, black front seat. Lying still, I would look back toward the window to watch the tall treetops sway.

In my mind I said, "Hello, Mr. Tree. How are you today? Please tell Miss Cloud where I am so she can pick me up."

With that simple fantasy, my mind managed to escape my body as it endured his painful pounding. "Raggy" stayed close, and my tears soaked her matted red hair. Cathy was also there. Her anger and loathing for The Monster intensified with each car ride. Even though she remained silent, I somehow felt protected in her presence.

The Monster repeatedly warned me not to tell anyone or he would kill me.

I was three, four, five, and then six years old. I believed him. Every time.

After bouts of belly pain and numerous urinary tract infections, our family pediatrician admitted me to the hospital in the spring of 1972. Tracy, my roommate, was older than me. Her mom sat bedside and brushed her hair. Since my mother worked full time and had seven other children, Mary was there for me instead, mimicking this maternal behavior by softly touching the red yarn on Raggy's head. Mary was so kind and gentle. She wore cozy sweaters. Her presence provided me comfort.

Just outside our room was a scratched, chrome and black pay phone. I often borrowed a stool from the nurses' station so I could pop a dime in and call my mother. Tracy was discharged before me, and although I was happy for her, it pained my heart to be left behind. Mary sensed my anxiety and cradled my little body.

While Tracy packed her bag, her mom walked over to me and placed her hand in mine before she left. I hugged Raggy close with one hand and gratefully squeezed my new roll of dimes from her in the other.

A few days and numerous tests later, doctors determined that my chronic urinary tract infections were the result of a "bubble bath allergy." Upon discharge from the hospital, the abuse coincidentally ceased. I did not tell anyone the truth, as The Monster had convinced me that no one would ever believe me.

I did, however, share my secret with the numerous "friends" I created who would support me in what would become my lifelong healing process.

Cathy and Mary were only the beginning of these alternative personalities, or "alters."

Due to the incessant, severe trauma that occurred at a young age, my little, developing brain could not process the pain alone. The alters became my complex coping strategy, allowing me to separate myself from the harrowing experiences. In time, I shifted subconsciously among the alters, depending on my life's circumstances.

According to the Cleveland Clinic, about 90 percent of cases of Dissociative Identity Disorder (DID)—which was previously called "multiple personality disorder"—involve some history of abuse. DID is usually a reaction to trauma. It's a coping mechanism to avoid bad memories associated with severe emotional, physical, and/or sexual abuse and is characterized by the presence of two or more distinct personality identities or alters. Each may have a unique name, personal history, and characteristics.

The Mayo Clinic says that personal identity is still forming during childhood, so a child is more able than an adult to step outside of himself or herself and observe trauma as though it's happening to a different person. A child who learns to dissociate in order to endure a traumatic experience might use this coping mechanism in response to stressful situations throughout life.

I was diagnosed with DID in the fall of 2018. Although I felt profound sadness, I also experienced relief.

Cathy, the bully I had created to fight the priest, had turned on me.

She was constantly nagging at me about my weight, my looks, and my life until her rage pushed for the final straw—my death. Cathy, the woman I had counted on to protect me, was now driving me to kill myself.

I sat in bed and cried and pleaded with her. "If I die, we all die."

One night after a movie, I went for a drive and ended up smoking Marlboros next to a dumpster in Cleveland. I was so confused and couldn't understand how I'd gotten there, and yet at the same time, it all felt so familiar. Fear took over, and I sought help.

I reached out to a Catholic nun whom I had met twenty years prior, and she connected me to a local therapist. My therapy sessions felt like a safe haven. Soft spoken and slight in stature, my therapist provided me the space I needed to release and explore all corners within my angst-filled body and mind.

For years, I bore the dark shame of a secret from my tormented childhood: sexual abuse at the hands of a religious figure and close family friend. During my late teens and early twenties, I suffered through bulimia, cutting, and an overall disdain for my body. At the age of thirty-two, I found the strength to start talking about everything that had happened to me.

Little by little, as if peeling the greens away from an ear of corn, I discovered the sweet gold—the light buried inside of me.

My father often said while teaching me to drive, "Don't look in the rearview mirror. The road is in front of you." His words ring true today. As a young child, I had been terrorized into remaining silent. Now I have broken through and, with faith, continue the healing path in front of me.

Through my deepest wounds and in my darkest days, I found a passion and purpose in providing kids the tools and teaching to improve their self-esteem. Creating IPride helped to heal my inner child of the shame and self-loathing I lived with throughout my life. IPride is a program that aligns with education-based core social and emotional learning competencies. It emphasizes mindfulness, creative thought, expression, and basic physical fitness. My IPride mantra is "Who can I serve today?"

Never had that mantra been more meaningful than in the summer of 2019.

Michelle and I met eleven years ago, when our sons were preparing to enter kindergarten. Both boys were apprehensive about starting school and had a preliminary meeting with the teacher to alleviate any anxiety.

Eventually, I would discover that Michelle suffers from *hereditary amyloidosis*, a rare genetic condition. Throughout her life, she'd been grimly aware of the potential diagnosis, as a number of her relatives had passed away at an early age from the disease. Like me, many of Michelle's friends were not aware of the extent of her illness.

In July 2019, Michelle shared with me that her life would soon depend on a kidney transplant. She asked if I would say a prayer for her to get placed on a transplant list.

"Of course I will pray for you. And when you do get put on the list, let me know. I will get tested to see if I'm a match."

The voice was all mine. The words, however, were distinctly Divine.

A couple of months later, science and faith joined forces, and Michelle was placed on a waiting list. It's rare for non-related individuals to be a kidney match, but my faith persisted, and I went through the testing process. On December 6, 2019, a woman from the Cleveland Clinic called and asked if Michelle was my sister. I replied, "No."

"Wow! You are 100 percent Michelle's match."

I was the only one tested.

At this point, Michelle's kidneys were still functioning enough to get by. By the time the transplant was scheduled, our sons were seniors in high school. The same two kids who met in kindergarten were points of light that connected their mothers to this destiny. I truly believe that I was born with Michelle's kidney and have served as its caretaker until God deemed it time.

Weeks away from surgery—or as I call it, a "transfer of life"—the surgeon determined that he could use the same incision that brought my oldest son into the world. How beautiful that my body has been blessed to provide life through the same opening twice.

Part of me has died. Another part, which I created, wanted to kill me. But today, the part of me that courageously fought to survive is extending the gift of life to another.

A Mother's Mission to Save Her Child
by Deborah Beauvais

I would imagine what the future would look like for my child.

Sometimes, in our dysfunctional relationship, I kept a low profile; other times, I spoke up. Sometimes it didn't matter. The abuse would come either way.

We had been arguing earlier. I was in the shower when my husband pulled the shower curtain over and hit me. While I had taken the emotional and physical abuse before and after we were married, I was in shock when it happened while I was pregnant with my first child.

Like many, my childhood was tumultuous and difficult.

I had little self-worth. My mom and dad didn't realize their constant, degrading words would make such an impression on a child, but when you hear "You're stupid" every day, it's only natural to believe it.

My mom had had her own tumultuous childhood, experiencing things no child should endure. Dealing with stress was very challenging for her. Keeping it together with five kids became unbearable, and she struggled with mental health issues and alcohol. I was a young teenager when she left our home, in the middle of the night, with some guy and my younger siblings. My sister and I stayed with our dad. I felt guilt when I realized that now, one of my other sisters would have to be the mom.

I met my first husband at a dance. At the beginning, it was fun and exciting. The criticism started soon into the relationship; jealously when I looked at another guy, or derogatory words about the way I dressed. At times like these, the abuse would accelerate. In a sense, for me, it just seemed natural to accept abuse. As many young women coming from a broken home, I thought when we got married, it would be different. But the truth is, the abuse got worse. Even though I knew it was wrong to hit another person, I understood why my husband was abusive. He was continuing the cycle of his father's abuse to his mother. He also had been on the receiving end of his father's rage.

I still thought I could fix everything, as I yearned for love and a wonderful marriage, like those I saw in the movies.

Instead, at nineteen, I got married and became a wife entrenched in a vicious cycle of abuse.

I made up stories that would explain the bruises and the black eye came from the kitchen cabinet door. When I became pregnant, I was so excited to be a mom, and I still believed everything would improve. Foolishly, I thought, "Certainly there wouldn't be any physical abuse while carrying my child."

When it did happen, that day in the shower, I was in shock. We were having a baby! How could he do this?

I made a vow that neither he nor anyone else would harm my child. From that day on, I knew there was no other choice but to leave, to protect my child. I was on a mission to keep my child safe.

I continued to work as a hairdresser/stylist and was able to save ten dollars here and there without it being noticed. For the next five months, I planned how I would run away. Legally, I knew I could take some items of furniture from the apartment. There was so much to figure out, yet I was driven to see it through.

During our marriage, as time went on, he would go on bouts of drinking and occasional trips with guy friends. When he'd return, I would do my best to keep a low profile. My friends said he was cheating on me; it really didn't matter anymore. To keep my inner strength up, I would imagine what the future would look like for my child.

I didn't have a place to go, but that didn't frighten me as much as staying with him.

My childhood experiences and learning to be independent helped me through this crisis. I thought about my mom a lot. I loved her unconditionally, but I wanted to do everything I could to *not* be like her. I wanted my children to feel loved and safe with a stable home.

It was time. The baby was coming. I was glad my husband wasn't around, as I didn't want him there. I asked a neighbor to take me to the hospital. It was a girl! After four days in the hospital, I came home with my baby daughter. A deep surge of love came over me, even though I felt totally overwhelmed. It took a month to recover from childbirth and get some strength back. As my husband continued to take off for days at a time, my plan was coming together.

He told me he'd be gone for the weekend. My daughter was six weeks old, and I was twenty-one when I packed up some things and ran away. It was frightening, exciting, and crazy at the same time. I wondered if he would return in the midst of my moving. My dad and a couple of friends came to help. Thank God no one, including the neighbors, told my husband.

While everything was being loaded up, my stepmother drove me around looking for an apartment to rent. I had saved $200; a friend gave me another $100. Back then, we depended on newspaper ads and word of mouth to find available rentals. When we found an opening, I would go the door or rental office with my baby and immediately be turned away. Nobody would rent to a woman with a child. One had to have a husband. In today's world, that sounds simply crazy, yet it was fact back then.

That weekend, we found an old place owned by an elderly woman who agreed to rent to me. I was elated as I signed the contract. I would find out later that there were two issues. One, I couldn't have more than two family members visit at one time. Two, an elderly woman in the apartment downstairs complained I was making too much noise in the middle of the night. The old, creaky floors were noisy as I walked across to feed my baby every three hours.

I bought an old car and kept my job, but with fewer hours. The salon owner was so kind and understanding. I tried to balance working at the salon, while my stepmother watched my daughter, being an at-home mother. The old car kept breaking down. It was a rough time, but I kept going.

I had to look for another place.

My stepmother and I were back to driving around looking for an apartment again. We looked everywhere, including five towns over. Each time, I was turned away because I didn't have a husband with me. Finally, after almost giving up, we came across the most wonderful woman who graciously rented to me—no husband needed. The two-floor home had been turned into four apartments dedicated to women with children. I was so grateful. I'll never forget her.

Unfortunately, my dad had said he would only move me once. It was upsetting at the time, but several other people stepped up, and in no time, my daughter and I were in our new, one-bedroom apartment. It was clean with lots of light. All the other women seemed as determined as I was to do the best they could for their children.

Instead of going into the salon, I started styling hair-wigs, which were popular back then. It wasn't enough to make ends meet, so I signed up for assistance. I was grateful, but I also felt a bit embarrassed, because of the stigma attached. I did what many mothers had to do. I made sure my daughter had formula, diapers, and food. There wasn't much left, so I ate a lot of cereal.

I became fearful when my husband found out where I was. I was uncomfortable daily, wondering what might happen. I filed for a divorce. Back then, the court system wasn't supportive to women—it was in favor of men. To make matters worse, I believe my father-in-law paid off the lawyer, so his son could get what he wanted—which was *not* his child or me, but revenge.

The divorce was final.

He was granted permission to see his daughter, but when he came to get her for the first time, I wouldn't open the door. Luckily, we didn't go back to court. It was at this time an acquaintance through our group of friends came home from overseas. He would bring food and gifts and we'd listen to records. Little did I know he would become my future husband.

Looking back, I realize now that I've been guided since I was a child. I was and am never alone. I've learned so much about my true self and I now value who I am. I've embraced the difficult times. I even see them as a gift to my being. I'm a brave, determined woman who can accomplish anything I put my mind and heart to.

I was on a mission to do everything possible for my daughter because I loved her so dearly. In the process of making a life for her, I saved my own.

Self-Love Paved the Way
by Diane Vich

I told my parents the story they could never have expected.

It was finally time for me to share my gut-wrenching story with my family. They had not been aware of my abuse as a child. It all began when I re-read my amazing story in the previous Sacred Stories of Transformation book, *Crappy to Happy.*

Forgotten memories and painful reality set in.

My difficult decision spun me into an emotional defense-mechanism: stress-induced amnesia. This survival mechanism began with me completely forgetting the story I had submitted to the book. Was it to avoid a conversation with my family that needed to occur? I could not discuss what I could not remember. Fortunately, my memory returned in time to make the shift into sharing my sordid story and healing my old wounds.

The moment I submitted my story for *Crappy to Happy*, my subconscious mind climbed aboard an emotional rollercoaster of doubt, guilt, shame, and fear. These memories began as Covid-19 stress was impacting my inner world and the world around me, as a nurse working through the pandemic.

As my complete amnesia of my story progressed, I balanced life as a Covid nurse, podcast host, and mom by focusing on self-love as much as I could through the torrential storms that arose in my home life, work, and the outer world. My amnesia also impacted the effectiveness and true power of my gift of "Orgazmik Healing," because the highly stressful situation impacted my libido.

Covid-19 pandemic stress also caused me to disconnect from all meaningful relationships, because the outer world became too much for me to process. I was still learning to overcome each obstacle that arose without completely falling apart emotionally. This meant I stopped calling friends and coworkers I used to see every day. With the collapse of my department in the hospital, all my friends who were also facing hard times didn't have my silly, funny, uplifting attitude to boost them during their tough times. It felt like I was juggling balls, and this one fell tumbling into a black hole, waiting for me to find it again.

Something was going to make me "wake up" in less than thirty days.

Fast forward to October 5, 2020. It began as a beautiful day filled with joy as my son turned fourteen years old. I was working virtually as a Covid nurse and never expected the text that was about to reach me.

As I was getting through a stressful and busy Monday's workload, a dreadful message from my brother came through my phone saying my cousin has suddenly passed away. I picked up the phone to hear the story and get the bad news in more detail.

In that moment, my day went from sunshine to deep darkness. My cousin, whom I loved dearly but had failed to contact during the

40

entire pandemic, had just passed away that morning from a pulmonary embolism. She had left behind her husband and fourteen-year-old son.

Emotions began to rush in. Not only was I thinking of her son and husband and their loss, but also of my own. I suddenly realized another ball had fallen in my juggling act, and this one wasn't coming back. How should I give this news to my son? I knew our family would be coming over for his fourteenth birthday dinner. I knew my cousin's death would come up in conversation.

The stress of the weeks of October was already testing me, and then *Crappy to Happy* was released on October 6. I was still publishing podcast interviews and pushing through grief while recording new ones. Thankfully, I had started therapy to work through my abuse a few weeks before my cousin's death—because at the funeral, I would come face-to-face with my abusers, when my grief and emotions were already raw.

I still hadn't shared my childhood abuse story with the rest of my family.

Now I had another obstacle in my path to speaking my truth about the abuse. How do you tell your parents of your abuse while they grieve? How do you tell your brother of your sexual childhood trauma while he grieves the loss of his cousin and coworker? At a time of death, how do you finally face that your story needs to be shared so you can live your purpose and change the world?

How do you work up the courage to share a secret you held for thirty-eight years?

Well, everything was meant to happen exactly as it did, because I needed a giant kick in the butt to get moving, and the dire situation did that for me. Externally, I focused on self-love and healing during the funeral. Internally, I dealt with my emotional thunderstorm.

The dreadful truth of my grief and heartache was about to become very clear. The *Crappy to Happy* book arrived, and I opened to my chapter to read my story, about which I had completely forgotten. I literally said out loud, "Oh shit! My parents have a copy, and I still haven't told them." I knew they were preoccupied with grief and imagined, or hoped, the book was probably sitting somewhere unopened.

But the book in my hand lit a fire in me to work up the courage to tell my story.

On the day of the funeral, a sense of release and pure love for my cousin swept over me. It was surreal to be so calm amidst all the stress and chaos this experience had caused to my body, mind, and psyche. But my focus on self-love was on overdrive. Each day included plenty of breaks for dancing, yoga, meditation, and yoni healing.

After the funeral, as we entered the car to return to our home, I saw a yellow butterfly, a sign of rebirth and renewal. My cousin was sending me a message. It was time for me to shine. It was time for me to tell my story. And I sensed my grandmothers, aunts, uncles, and cousin were there to support me on the journey. I knew there were angels watching over me, even in the dark times.

During all this stress, I had been teaching my "7 Day Stress Cleanse" course, and I knew it was time for me to use this technique for myself, to prepare for my next healing step... the release from the cocoon of suppressed child abuse. It was ironic, because I always tell people, "If you have a big event or stressful task coming up, prepare yourself with a deep self-love cleanse." Now I needed one big time!

I took a week off from work to be with my husband for our anniversary and I prepared myself to tell my family upon my return. And that is precisely what I did. We went away for a few days to our home in the Keys, where I could practice all my self-loving tools and prepare for the biggest conversation of my life. Thankfully, it landed on the perfect time of the moon cycle, the waxing moon. My energy boost and motivation were on point. My week of self-love paved the way for courage, compassion, and truth.

I told my parents the story they could never have expected.

They were both shocked by my truth, but they began to put the pieces together as we spoke. My parents realized my learning disabilities had started in kindergarten, right after my abuse began. They realized that all my digestive issues, headaches, and hair loss began after the trauma took over. And they began to understand a little more clearly why their daughter had completely shifted her life in these very strange ways of alternative healing.

But when they asked me why I was sharing my story now—and in a book, for everyone to read, so many years later—I answered, "I just knew I had to tell my story so I could support children facing hardships they also couldn't emotionally comprehend, especially when they emerge from being locked down with their abusers. I will be here for them."

And I would also be here to help women reconnect with their inner goddess through sacred sexual healing. As the holiday stresses continued and I shared my story with those in my family, I continued my self-loving routine and therapy.

Leading by example, I began preparation to teach other women what had helped me heal: "Orgazmik-Meditation" and "Orgazmik-Healing", which shares the power of conscious orgasms to release trauma from the body, mind, and psyche. The technique moved me through some difficult times over the holidays, like when I experienced a back injury after a confrontation on Thanksgiving Day. During this time, and as part of my growth process, I chose to take a break from my podcast to truly teach and make a difference in this world. And this space helped me pick up one of the balls I had dropped. I began reconnecting with colleagues who were facing their own hardships to provide cheerful uplifting support.

The long and often painful journey brought me to my miracle and true mission.

What began with my campaign to help kids with hardships, using my daily mindfulness practices, became a way to heal my inner child. And since my little girl is still scared to share her story of sexual healing, I am still supporting her by focusing my attention between giving back and teaching. Being selfless helps me focus on others' needs as I work up my courage to speak my truth to the world.

Now it is 2021, and I am in the middle of a moon cycle, recording videos for my class to help women during the chaotic mood shifts that occur as our bodies feel the moon's impact on the outer world. The classes are recorded when the mood is right, the moon is supportive, and the sexual healing is aligned.

And my healing has finally allowed me to work up the courage to write again. I am in the middle of writing another erotic novel under my alias, as well as a book to help men understand the complexities a Goddess faces in this patriarchal society as she transcends the obstacles life brings, to find her true essence, purpose, and passions in the world.

The world has brought many opportunities for me to evolve and grow, to fully reach my soul's purpose. My mayhem did not destroy me. It was cathartic and it made me stronger. And that is one of my many miracles.

Spiritual Flat Tires
by Bernie Siegel, MD

*The meaning my life takes on relates to choosing life
and who or what I see as my Lord.*

I was being driven to the airport by a nice lady who had attended my lecture—when lo and behold, one of the tires on the vehicle suddenly deflated.

"A flat tire is not what I need when I'm trying to make a tight flight!" I said to myself. I told her to get the jack and I would change the tire.

"I'm sorry, my husband has the jack in his car," she answered.

While we stood waiting for help from anyone at all, a young man drove up. When he learned what our problem was, he quickly changed the tire, and we went on our way. However, when we arrived at the airport, we learned I had missed my flight by only a few minutes. My reaction was not a happy one… until I learned the flight I missed had crashed after taking off.

Thank God for flat tires. They make you wonder about the meaning of life.

Life, in and of itself, has no meaning. It is simply a mechanical event. But I believe life presents us with the opportunity and physical ability to be creative and connect with our Lord and the process of creation, to create a meaningful life.

If I were provided with a perfect world, there would be no place for creation or meaning. The world would simply be a magic trick. The meaning of life comes from how I use my mind and body and whether I contribute to, or become destructive to, the process of creation. When I have the opportunity to choose from what is placed before me—life and death, good and evil—meaning arises. The meaning my life takes on relates to choosing life and who or what I see as my Lord.

My Lord can be material things and selfish choices based upon my desires and feelings, or it can be a chance to love the world, and our neighbors, when I have the right Lord.

Choosing life means I choose life-enhancing behavior for all living things through my actions and behavior. Then my life takes on meaning.

I symbolically represent the same opportunities and elements as a satellite dish, a remote control, and a TV screen. A satellite dish has access to many channels and programs, and with my remote control, I can select which channel I tune into and watch the program displayed.

The problem is, there are many Lords out there for me to choose from, like all the channels available to me and the remote control. My mind is like the remote. It chooses what it tunes into and what it is exposed to and learns about life and meaning. Then my body, like the TV screen, displays which Lord and programs I have been watching and learning from, and thus my life and activities take on meaning.

If my Lord is the "Lord of Revenge"—because of a life experience of indifference, rejection, and abuse instead of love—then the meaning of my life will be totally destructive, as all the headlines reveal. But when I realize we are all here to contribute love to the world—in a way personally selected, and not one imposed upon me—then life takes on meaning and becomes a joyful experience, no matter what profession or lifestyle I choose.

Thus, I have learned that the meaning of life is to give each human being the opportunity to live a genuine and authentic life dedicated and devoted to life-enhancing behavior.

When I submit to what others impose upon me, I lose my life and its meaning.

But when I abandon my untrue selves and tune in to the "Lord of Love Channel," every action I take is authentic, meaningful, life-saving, and life-enhancing for all living things of every species residing on this planet we all call home. That makes God happy.

And when God is happy, miracles happen—like flat tires.

Now, getting back to flat tires… A few years later, history repeated itself again; a flat tire, a woman driver, and no jack in the car to change it. But now, because of my previous experience of missing my plane, which saved my life, I have faith. And sure enough, a young man pulled off the road, learned about my problem, and quickly changed the tire like a professional. This time, we made the flight and had no problems. But that was just the beginning of the real story.

As we settled into our seats on the plane, it was announced that there was a blizzard in Canada at the city where I was to lecture. A voice came over the PA system and asked passengers to volunteer to cancel their flight so the plane would have sufficient fuel to reach another safe and secure airport. Many chose to deplane.

My wife and I, and another couple, were the only passengers who didn't get off the plane, but we were concerned about missing our connecting flight. As we took off, we all became family and chatted. That is when I was relieved to learn that our pilot was also the pilot of our connecting flight—so despite the delay created by the passengers who volunteered to cancel their flight, the airlines would have to hold the connecting plane for him when we landed.

It sounded like another miracle.

Once we landed at the airport, I was told by the airline attendant who greeted our plane that our connecting flight had departed. I announced that it had not—since the pilot of that flight was with me. The airline agents all quickly learned I was sober and correct.

God and I had done it again! There are no coincidences. When you live in your heart and choose your course in life, miracles happen.

Final Thoughts

From Kat's dream lover, to mental illness and substance and sexual abuse, to watching mayhem in daily life repeat itself, the hope for a better life prevails. The thread that ran through all the stories in this section was how no one had to face their mayhem alone. The right person, such as a good friend or future husband, always showed up at the right time. In the stories, hope connected hearts and healed emotions. Hope was the antidote to life's mayhem. A mother's love was often the answer to unspoken questions. Self-love often paved the road to miracles. As Bernie so aptly wrote, "When God is happy, miracles happen."

PART 2
HEALTH AND WELL-BEING
I'll Stand by You

There is a me that is perfect and whole.

Wounds

by Rev. Ariel Patricia

The change I was experiencing was a blessing.

My life wasn't perfect, but as life does, it continued. I was becoming more and more confused as to what my feelings were toward my husband. Longing for that personal, adult male connection, I started to feel trapped in my marriage. However, I still had a very strong sense of commitment to our family unit. I wasn't going to do anything to jeopardize the family—even if it meant sacrificing my own personal happiness.

My life wasn't perfect, but it was enough.

However, within a few months, I knew in my heart that my husband and I were further apart emotionally than even I could accept or ignore any longer. I had to address it, but I had to do it carefully. I wanted to make sure he understood that I still loved him; we just needed to work on some things. I believed it would make both of us happier.

I found some time one night after dinner. We had just finished cleaning up the kitchen and were standing by the counter. The mood was relaxed, and we had some privacy; our girls busy working on their homework upstairs. It seemed as good a time as any.

I took a deep breath and blurted out, "I think we are not as close as married people should be."

He looked at me a little quizzically, as if he didn't understand what he had just heard. Then his face relaxed and a look of release washed over it. His response shocked me to my core.

"I agree," he said with relief. "I haven't loved you for a long time. I was just pretending."

"What? What did you just say?" I stammered, feeling as if I couldn't catch my breath.

His words were suffocating. Motionless, I stood there while a torrent of emotions raged inside of me. I looked into the eyes of the person I thought I knew completely, the partner I had trusted without question. A cold, damp feeling of dread came over me. He was the person I thought loved me unconditionally, the one that I had built my life with.

What did he just say?

I wasn't expecting flowers and chocolates, but I wasn't expecting this response, either. I was expecting more along the lines of, "I agree. I feel it, too. What can we do about it?"

Astonished and numb, I pleaded for some explanation. He had none. He said he would have gone on pretending forever, but since I had the courage to bring it up, he was able to finally be honest.

We briefly tried marriage counseling, but his mind was made up. He didn't love me. He was sorry. He felt guilty for the pain he was causing the girls and me. But he didn't love me.

We were divorced within the year.

Everyone marveled at how civil we were and how well I was handling everything. I went into survival mode during the divorce proceedings. I had to protect my children emotionally. All my strength went into doing that. I had to stay calm. I knew they were watching me. I tried not to argue. I tried to act normally. Really, I tried.

I also had to financially protect myself and my children. There were so many things to think about. How could I stay in the house with the kids? They were in high school by then, and I didn't want to uproot them. How could I pay for college? We were just getting by with two salaries and one house. How could I make this work?

We eventually figured the financial part out. In comparison to the rest, that turned out to be the easy part.

He moved out, we got divorced, and then I fell apart.

This experience exposed some deep wounds.

I had wounds that for many years had been scabbed over. Deep, thick scabs protected me and allowed me to pretend they weren't there. Now, without warning, they had been ripped wide open.

Wounds are funny things. We all have them. We respond from them, sometimes consciously, but many times not. They affect our thoughts and behaviors even when we're not aware of it. If we look closely, we can even see the wounds of others in their actions.

Some wounds can lie dormant for many years and only return to taunt us when we are faced with the very thing that wounded us. And the funniest thing of all is that wounds don't heal on their own, regardless of how much we pretend they are not there. We must heal them ourselves.

My personal wounds had to do with self-love and my relationships with others. And they were much deeper than I had ever realized. When they resurfaced, I was surprised not only by their presence, but by their intensity.

My wounds surprised people. Most people considered me to be a smart, attractive, capable woman with many accomplishments in my life. "Capable" is a nice way to say assertive, or opinionated, or a take-charge kind of woman.

But there was also another side to me that had deep-rooted feelings of not being "good enough" or not being "worth the effort." My thoughts would go something like: "I'm pretty, just not pretty enough. I'm thin, just not thin enough."

I'm smart, but intelligence wasn't something celebrated in a girl growing up during the '60s and '70s. We were told to make sure we weren't smarter than our future husbands, because men didn't find smart women attractive—and God forbid, of all things, don't be capable.

But the traits not celebrated were the things I clung to.

I believed they were all I had to offer. I was the smart and capable one. My intellect and the sheer force of my will allowed me to succeed in most endeavors. I became goal-oriented and proved my worth by accomplishing my goals. I never allowed myself to fail, because I believed success was the only thing that validated me.

That, however, didn't translate into healthy personal relationships. Because I didn't find value in myself as a whole person, I never believed that the whole of me could be embraced, cherished, and loved. I was only the "smart" and "capable" one.

Now officially alone, I was confronted with all these old feelings. My husband's rejection confirmed, in the most painful way, what I had always thought deep down about myself. I wasn't worth it.

The next few months were hard, very hard. I tried to come to grips with my merciless and unending questions. What was wrong with me? Why wasn't I worth fighting for? Why was I so easy to just walk away from?

I cried every day. I cried even when I didn't know what I was crying about. There seemed to be an unending supply of sadness that kept welling up inside of me. I felt like my body was trying to expel the sadness with deep sobs. But another sob always followed, more painful than the last.

Sunday nights were especially hard. That was garbage night. Besides everything else I had to deal with, that was the night that I had to take the garbage to the street. It was just a routine chore on my never-ending list of chores, but it signified the cold slap of reality that I was alone because I was unlovable.

I didn't know what to do. People told me I was falling into a depression and that I should see a therapist. It seemed so overwhelming. It was all I could do to handle my day-to-day responsibilities, let alone make any more changes.

Then one day, to my surprise, a very large toad came to visit me…

I woke up to a warm spring morning, the kind of morning that captures each of your senses, where a bird's conversation wakes you up and a sliver of sunlight shining through your blinds draws you to your window. Opening the window, a warm breeze greets your hands first, then your arms, then your face. The breeze carries in the sweet, mixed aroma of earth, plants, and springtime air. It was the kind of morning you wish you could freeze in time, so you could escape into its vitality and promise forever.

Lately, I had been wishing I could escape to somewhere. But it's hard to escape when you're living with your deeply embedded wounds. So, I stretched one more time and forced myself out of bed. It seemed I had to do that more and more often, too.

As I stood up, I noticed an unfamiliar shape on my headboard. It was right above where I had just been sleeping. I knew that because I was still keeping to my side, not comfortable claiming the entire bed as my own yet. The shape was dark and round, I thought it was a rock. Sighing, I rubbed the sleep out of my eyes, and wondered how in the world a rock got on top of my headboard. As I reached my hand out to grab it, I was stopped short as my eyes finally realized what it was. It wasn't a rock. It was a huge, living, breathing toad, dirty brown and covered in warts. Unmoving, it stared at me with its dull, dark eyes.

I was speechless. The toad was larger than my fist—too large to have come in on someone's clothes. I stared at it incredulously and then started to freak out a little bit. Okay, I freaked out a lot.

"Megan! Get up! I need your help!" I yelled, abruptly waking one of my daughters.

"What?" she yawned, coming out of her bedroom.

"Look at my bed! Get it off for me!" I implored her.

"Oh my God! I'm not touching that!" she responded quickly.

"Please, you have to! I can't do it!" I pleaded, feeling vulnerable and overwhelmed once again.

Now I don't know if it's because Megan is such a good kid, or if she knew that I was too emotionally fragile to deal with this intruder, but Megan handled it. She had the presence of mind to get a big plastic cup

60

and she gently maneuvered the toad into it, then carried it outside and let it go safely in the woods.

How bizarre! How in the world did this large, fat toad get into the house unnoticed—and then hop up a flight of stairs and down a hall, find my room, and make his way onto my headboard? And how did I not hear it or feel it? This toad had a message for me!

There are multiple messages when a toad visits you.

One is a message about amphibians. Amphibians are very adaptable to their surroundings. They are cold-blooded and use their environment as their heat source. Amphibians also go through a process of metamorphosis. Toads change from an egg, to a tadpole, to a toad, and then they periodically shed their skin.

If an amphibian is your totem, the message is one of adaptability and significant personal change or rebirth. You can experience a major shift or transformation. Questions to ask yourself may include: "What is changing in my life? How can I adjust to new situations? What do I have to shift to embrace this transformation?"

Perfect, I thought, disheartened and longing for some peace of mind. Here was another message about change and rebirth. Okay, okay. If I was going through a metamorphosis from my old self to a new self, then I needed to get a grip and adapt to my changing circumstances.

I had to trust that my new self was going to be happier and more pulled-together than my current self. I hoped the change would hurry, because this was hard! Unfortunately, I couldn't just sleep until the change took place. I had to live through each part of it—warts, and all.

The messages specifically from a toad's appearance are about self-examination and good luck. "What is really going on with me? What do

I fear? Is my fear hindering my progress?" These were all questions to ask myself. However, my emotions were still too raw to supply the answers. They would have to wait.

I found some comfort in the message of good luck. I believed it meant the change I was experiencing was a blessing, and that my life would get better. I knew that God was confirming that He would never give me more than I could handle—and He was right.

No One Will Take My Child
by Peggy Willms

I thanked God for giving me the strength to walk the ten-year path.

While I sat perched on the crisp-papered patient exam table, my slightly balding physician and his nurse embarked on a combative verbal war.

"Run the test again, Sandy!"

"I already did. She's pregnant."

Were they talking about me? Surely not me! That wasn't the reason for my visit! I couldn't be pregnant!

I had no intention of having a baby—at least not now. I was a wife, the mother of a six-year-old, and had just competed at Ms. Fitness Nationals. I held two jobs, taught dozens of fitness classes, and trained dozens of clients each week.

There was no room in my life for a baby!

It was the Summer of 1993, and I had just arrived home from a camping trip. Catching up on household responsibilities, I decided to go through the mail. An envelope from the local blood bank stood out. I casually

63

opened it, not knowing how the words inside would forever change my world.

My donation had been denied due to a detection of Hepatitis C. They recommended I contact my physician for further instructions. Further instructions? For what? I didn't even know what Hep C was. With no search engines or smart phones back then, and not knowing if I should tell anyone, I sat spinning in the longest weekend of my life.

It took more than a week to get an appointment with my doctor, a visit I will never forget. I entered the office as a got-her-shit-together, fit chick and left a blubbering, dirty disaster, denying I was a druggy or a sleaze and having to prove I had no tattoos. Oh yea, I also left with a referral to an Ob-Gyn. I was confused and horrified and plagued with questions. I was so upset that the receptionist had to drive me home.

How did I get Hepatitis C? It took me ten years to figure it out, but I did! And it almost cost my son his life.

The next few weeks consisted of testing my oldest son and his dad. Both were negative. Little was known about this diagnosis then, and I had few answers I could share about how I contracted it. Though many had opinions to share.

"Pregnancy is taxing on the body and its organs. It could be very risky for both you and the baby as it is. Hep C is a blood disorder that directly affects the liver. You really need to think about your options."

"Options? Are you saying, terminate the pregnancy? No!"

It was Groundhog Day.

I had the same conversation with everyone in my life. They would say, "Why take the risk? What if you die? What if the baby has something wrong with him/her and no mother? What if you both die? What about Shane (my oldest son)? What if..."

The confusion and fear were unfathomable. Hep C had only been in discussion about four years prior and little was known about its true causes or effects.

I couldn't celebrate the pregnancy. After all, it was my fault I had this damn disease, even though I still had no idea how and when I'd contracted it. Day after day, I was reminded that I was risking my life and the baby's. I carried around the burden of this diagnosis and the burden of the risks to move forward.

I succumbed to the pressure of those around me.

I made an appointment at the abortion clinic. It was one of the most shameful experiences of my life, like sneaking into the dark alley of hell. Even the nurse looked at me sideways as she guided me into a room to watch the required "extraction" video. As the video rolled, I nearly vomited and raced out of the clinic.

After all, I was pro-life! My mother had become pregnant with me at fifteen. She chose to keep me. She could have easily had an abortion, stayed in school, and avoided the town's ridicule—but she didn't. And there I was, watching an end-of-life video that tore at my very heart and soul. My heart made the decision: I would leave and fight the fight, even if it was alone. From that moment on, I never looked back.

I had the greatest pregnancy.

I was the epitome of health, except for my afternoon ritual of a Twix bar and Coke. I never stopped weight training, teaching aerobics, or personally training clients. I was still leg pressing around 300 pounds into my seventh month. I even modeled in a bridal show.

Around Christmas time, we found out we were having a boy, and it didn't take long to agree his name would be Tanner Jordan. I finished out the pregnancy on the normally expected, mom-to-be track with baby showers, due-date guessing games, Lamaze classes, selecting godparents, prepping a nursery, and nesting. I had a feeling I would deliver him two weeks early, as I had his brother, and I did. A bouncing 7.5 pound baby boy.

Through the excitement of the pregnancy, my Hep C worry waned but never fully disappeared, I just had something more fun to focus on. The stress and worry came back full force when, on the day Tanner was born, the lactation nurse came in for a visit. She read my chart and dashed out of the room, only to return and inform me I could not breastfeed my baby.

"Oh, dear. I am so sorry, but you have Hepatitis C, and you cannot risk giving this disease to your child. Though the experience isn't quite the same, he will get the nutrients he needs with formula."

I was devastated.

This was yet another jab in my heart. I was determined his formula feeding wouldn't affect our bond. And after two days at the hospital, we headed home to begin our "normal" life as a family of four. Six days later, that all changed.

At two a.m. on March 23, 1994, our Little Man, as we called him, began making deep, moaning sounds. He had been in and out of fevers the previous day. I also had noticed his skin seemed to be darkening. By 7:30 a.m., my oldest son and I were racing to the ER.

I remember standing at the door of the lab, my head spinning as my seven-year-old was perched over his brother, astonished at the number of vials of blood being taken. I don't even remember how we got from the ER to the Peds floor. Through the chaos, doctors took spinal taps and placed IVs in my son's skull. There were relentlessly ringing phones and alarms.

Tanner's physician asked me to sit in the rocking chair and placed him in my arms. His body was riddled with cords. She knelt down beside me and calmly said, "I want you to hold him closely and calm him down. He is going to start having seizures. Support his head. Though we don't know how long they will last, he will come out of the episodes, but there may be a lot of them."

I remember looking in her eyes and asking if he was going to be alright, and she stood and simply replied, "I will be back soon."

At that exact time, I realized I hadn't yet cried. My first gigantic tear dropped onto my son's cheek. I heard his doctor being paged to the front desk, which was only twenty feet from our room. I heard her repeat back the test and the number. With my medical background, I knew the results were not good. His white blood cell count was over 50,000, which meant he had a severe infection.

Within minutes, I learned my baby boy—the one I had chosen not to terminate months ago, because of my Hepatitis C—now had Group B Spinal Meningitis and was fighting for his life.

My parents arrived within an hour to take my oldest son to their home, and as we were getting them ready to leave, Tanner's alarms started to blare. As if out of a movie scene, the staff started hollering and then whisked my baby out of my arms. Within a nanosecond, a red Tim the Toolman cart rolled in. The next thing I knew, the room was empty, and I was left not knowing where my baby went or what was happening.

There is nothing more difficult than seeing your children hurt.

It's hardest to see them hurt and knowing you can do absolutely nothing to help them. There were days I was allowed to touch his hand and rock him. There were days I was told I couldn't, as they thought I made him more upset. I think he was simply begging me to help him. One strategy proved successful. I was asked to wear a bandana on my chest for twenty-four hours. They placed it under his head in the incubator and my scent seemed to bring him comfort.

After his ten-day hospital visit, we were able to bring him home. That was even more joyful than the day he was born. If you're thinking, *Que sera*, they all lived happily ever after—No! You are so very wrong.

In less than a week, Tanner relapsed. Though he was still on antibiotics, his fevers returned. After a five-day hospital stint, I was starting to feel like this was the worst joke ever. But by the end of April, we were back home and settled in.

How did my Hep C journey turn out?

In 2003, my doctors were investigating some auto-immune issues I had been experiencing. A new provider decided to run a full panel of blood tests, one of which was for the Hepatitis C antibody. Though I'd had more than forty liver function tests in a decade, no one had ever re-checked the antibody levels.

The Godliest day of my life arrived. In July of 2003, I left my doctor's office with the news that I *didn't* actually have Hep C. They found no evidence of antibodies for that disease at all. The test results from a decade earlier most likely had been false-positive, as many of them were in the early days of detecting the disease.

68

My eyes gushed with disbelief as I drove home to an empty house. I raced into Tanner's room, fell to my knees, and smashed his sheets into my face, breathing in my now ten-year-old son's scent. I thanked God for giving me the strength to walk the ten-year path, which at times felt like it was a path I walked alone.

I had nearly ended my child's life; was told not to nurse him; and then spent a decade feeling ashamed and burdened with a disease *I never had*. As I relive this journey, my son, Tanner Jordan, has just had a son of his own, Crew Cole, born nearly twenty-seven years to the day after his father.

I dedicate this story of love to my first grandson, whose life would not have been possible if God had not given me the strength to trudge through the pregnancy and birth of his father. I thank my son, Tanner, for the strength that helped him endure, never giving up on himself or me.

A Christmas Gift Mantra
by Mary Ellen Lucas

I leaned toward the healing grace and the awareness
that everything was okay.

The lure of brightly-wrapped presents sat under the Christmas tree and stockings filled-to-the-brim hung from the fireplace mantle. All looked mighty tempting and inviting for my three young kids, who were eager to swoop into the fun of Christmas. In a rush to get to Mass early enough to get seats, I promised presents would be opened right after church. A busy day ahead for sure! Attendance at Mass for Christmas, all together as a family, would be a wonderful way to begin the day.

We dashed out the door and happiness welled within my heart. We arrived early enough to find seats for my husband, my two sons, my daughter, and I to be able to sit together. It was rare, especially on a holiday, to find seating. We made our way to one of the open pews in the front rows and settled in. It wasn't my first choice to sit in the front, but I was grateful we didn't have to stand—plus, what a bonus to be able to sit together!

Soon after Mass started, my oldest son, Sean, had a grand mal seizure.

In our family, Sean having a seizure wasn't out of the norm. His first grand mal seizure happened when he was ten-and-a-half-months old. More seizure types developed, and from then on, seizures became a part of Sean's life. I wouldn't say any of us had gotten used to witnessing a seizure, but we had more experience than most people. Watching Sean have a seizure was still hard for us to witness, let alone for others to see. It's an alarming sight. It can be frightening if one doesn't know what is happening.

The grand mal—or generalized tonic-clonic seizure—was the most frequent type Sean endured. Often, before this type of seizure, Sean would let out an awful scream. When Sean yelled during the Mass, I knew a seizure would follow. Sean lost consciousness as his body stiffened and contracted. As the seizure progressed, convulsive jerks began and he flailed about. I sat down, trying to hold onto Sean the best I could. The only thing I could do was to make sure Sean stayed free from injury. I kept him safe and waited for the seizure to pass.

Waiting for a seizure to end seems to take an interminable length of time. After a couple of minutes, Sean became limp and unresponsive as a state of disorientation began. This typically lasted a couple of more minutes. I spoke softly and gently to Sean to reassure him. I kept telling him he was okay, it was okay. The seizure exhausted Sean. Most likely, for the rest of day, he wouldn't have the same pep he normally would have.

Sitting in one of the front pews meant Sean's scream was heard by the congregation and the subsequent seizure caught the attention of everyone who was near us, including the priest. Despite my inner quaking, I maintained a calm demeanor throughout, hoping that others would be reassured that this wasn't the emergency it looked like. I did notice the priest had momentarily turned to look our way. Thankfully, he continued saying Mass. No one in our proximity did anything or said anything to us about what they saw.

I felt embarrassed to have our family noticed by the priest and some of the parishioners, but it couldn't be helped. It certainly wasn't the first time I would ignore stares from others.

For the duration of the Mass, I remained seated so I wouldn't disturb Sean, who was cradled in my lap, sleeping soundly. I completely checked out from whatever was happening in the service and got lost down the rabbit hole of my distracted thoughts. I was so disappointed and sad for Sean that he'd had a seizure on Christmas, of all days. Sean loved Christmas, like every child does. I knew that, more than likely, he wouldn't be able to fully enjoy opening his Christmas gifts, nor would he be fully present to the rest of the family.

One of the hardest things about a seizure disorder is its out-of-the-blue unpredictability.

Because of Sean's seizures, I was often in a hyper-alert state, on the lookout for signs of trouble. In the aftermath, I looked for answers, a search that was usually futile. However, it didn't stop me from constantly scanning for a potential explanation of what could have precipitated a seizure. I was ensnared in my thoughts as I searched for a logical explanation. What could have brought on this particular grand mal seizure—in church, no less? Perhaps the anticipation and excitement over Christmas was too much, and Sean's brain wiring short-circuited? Or had I put too much stress on Sean as I hurried him through the getting-ready routine earlier in the morning?

The priest began the homily, and I half-heartedly began to listen. He relayed the Nativity story, and his words were a backdrop to the sadness and disappointment I was feeling that Sean's Christmas was now spoiled. The priest talked about how Mary had to undertake an arduous journey. She had to travel into new territory. After arriving in Bethlehem, all the rooms were filled. No one readily offered support to Mary and Joseph. The only place available was a stable, where Mary gave birth to Jesus—or so the story goes. Surely, not the ideal conditions for any mother-to-be. The priest talked on.

The soothing tone of his voice began to calm me. I became more drawn into the story he was telling. For the first time that day, I gave the Mass my full attention. I felt he was speaking just to me. As I continued to watch him, it was clear the priest was speaking to the whole congregation until he came to a phrase that was like a refrain he repeated. When he spoke the phrase, he deliberately turned to face me. His eyes looked straight into my eyes as he said calmly, in a reassuring voice, about whatever was happening to Mary,

"It was okay."

Mary's faith helped her to know that no matter the circumstances, "It was okay." The peacefulness of his voice and the message of his words began to settle deeper within me. For a long time, my devotion to Mother Mary had been strong. In fact, Sean was born on one of her feast days. I could remember that, when I was still in the hospital after giving birth to Sean, I had a strong sense that Sean was Mary's child just as much as he was my son.

I met the eyes of the priest every time he looked at me. The oft-repeated refrain "It was okay" sure seemed to be a message he wanted to convey to me. But what did "it was okay" really mean? Didn't the definition of the word *okay* mean all is well or satisfactory? Was it an implication of assent and acceptance? I failed to understand how Mary could feel "okay" about the circumstances around Jesus's birth.

I tried to center myself to contemplate Mary's example. She had undertaken an arduous journey, not by choice. Sean's seizure disorder had taken us on a journey we had never planned. Mary didn't have any discernible future guarantees that everything would work out. Was Mary's faith so strong that she still believed that everything unfolded as it was meant to?

Our family didn't have any guarantees as to what would happen for Sean in the future. Medical experts we had consulted agreed that Sean most likely would continue having seizures and a shortened life span. At an earlier time, while seeking help from different neurologists, one doctor had given us a prognosis that I had banked my hopes on: Sean would continue to develop "normally."

However, since we couldn't stop the seizures, the damage had already begun to take its toll on his development. Along with less-than desirable medication side effects, the pronouncement the doctor had made proved to be grossly incorrect. There was no way I could prepare for what was to come.

I already felt beleaguered by the multiple emergency-room visits of the past.

Dealing with Sean's overwhelming medical condition often made me feel alone. There weren't any easy and readily available answers. Amazingly, Sean's first of many emergency overnight hospital stays happened after I returned home from Mass on another one of Mary's Feast Days. Would

I ever be able to be like Mother Mary and find a way to feel okay about what was happening? My churned-up thoughts persisted throughout the Mass.

As the priest held my gaze, his "It's okay" reassurances began to make an imprint. The tension I held in my body began to soften. The mystery of what was happening during Mass, on this Christmas morning, while Sean slept on my lap, didn't make any logical sense. Yet somehow, the message of "okay-ness" landed right in my heart. I accepted it as a truth.

For a few moments, I closed my eyes and chose not to pursue the pressing need to have Sean's challenges figured out. Even though my mother's heart ached for Sean, as it did whenever he seized, the message was weaving deeper into my heart. There, it reverberated until my heartache was eased. I leaned toward the healing grace and the awareness that everything was okay.

Weren't those the very words I had said to Sean, to ease and comfort him after he had the seizure? Perhaps I needed to receive this message, too. It was okay.

What a beautiful Christmas gift… a holy moment of peaceful awareness, knowing not only was it okay, but everything is okay.

Miracle Maker
by Dr. Anne Worth

As I exited the treatment center, a sign on the wall declared:
"You are a miracle."

escending the steep airplane stairs into the glare of an Arizona August afternoon, the asphalt heat hit me like a furnace blast. Heading into the terminal, I expected to see a uniformed chauffeur, or at least someone with a crisp, white shirt and a black tie, holding a placard with my name.

When I saw that the hand-printed sign announcing my arrival was held by a lanky old guy in a straw, sweat-stained cowboy hat and scuffed cowboy boots, I was a bit miffed. At the cost of laying out a grand a day, I expected a little more. Maybe not a brass band or a dozen roses, but possibly a long, black limousine?

Instead, I was herded into a minivan with a few other hot and sweaty souls. One couldn't fail to notice the facility's name plastered in big letters on the side of the vehicle.

So much for anonymity!

Our destination was an old dude ranch, secluded in the Arizona mountains. In its day, it had been famous as a gathering place for the elite. Now it was a ranch for dudes and gals with drinking problems… and other problems caused by the merry-go-round of addiction.

As we drove through the impressive twin stone pillars at the entrance to the treatment center, a sign on the wall proclaimed, "Expect a miracle." I sure needed a miracle, but after trying every treatment I could find for forty years, I didn't expect to find it here or anywhere else.

The staff greeted me cordially and escorted me to a room off the main lobby. Looking back, I saw the driver laboring to carry my bags, novels, and tennis racket to some unknown location. I assumed he was taking them to my room, but I didn't see those books or that tennis racket again for forty days!

In a little room, they examined every physical item I'd brought with me, practically strip-searching me. My Gucci leather tennis shoes were replaced with non-descript slippers and I was handed a blue lab coat to wear to identify me as a new patient.

I was enraged at being treated like a street junkie.

"Whoa! Wait a minute."

They ignored my concerns, whisked me into the detox unit, and repeated the words I was to hear over and over for the next forty days: "Trust the process."

When I tried to sleep the nightmare away, I was constantly interrupted by blood pressure readings and questions about my life. They gave me something to read called the "Big Book," which I assumed was a Bible—I left it unopened, further convinced I was in the wrong place.

By the third day, claustrophobic and nearly panicked, I was finally sprung from solitary detox into the community of the facility. Thank God! Maybe someone would listen to my grievances.

They assigned a "buddy" to show me around. Every time I complained about some aspect of the program, she just smiled and nodded. She seemed unnaturally cheerful and accepting of everything about the program, regardless of my agitation. *Look out for the Kool-Aid,* I thought.

My buddy escorted me to my new room, where I thought I would finally have some privacy. There were two beds and one bathroom.

"No way! This is too much!" I cried, demanding a private room. "I am not paying a thousand dollars a day to share a bathroom and sleep in the same room with some addict."

My buddy smiled and handed me a packet of stapled pages that listed the rules, regulations, schedules, and appointments. It made me furious. I was a desperate woman looking for medical help, not jail. Where were the movie stars I heard came here? Would they put up with this kind of treatment? I couldn't ask them—because there wasn't one in sight.

I wasn't an alcoholic, a drug addict, a love addict, or any other of their other labels.

It was clear that I ate too much; the scale had let that cat out of the bag. Overeating was at the top of my addiction list. I guess if you vacuumed too much, a 12-Step program could help you stop that, too.

On practically every inch of wall space in the facility, large signs displayed and discussed the 12 Steps *ad nauseam.* The first three steps stated we needed God because we are powerless over our lives.

No! No! And hell no! Could I sue the facility for pretending to be a hospital when it was some kind of religious cult?

The idea of depending on God was so objectionable to me, I thought there was no way I could get past it. The word *God* triggered a frightening memory of when I was a little four-year-old girl.

I loved spending time with my grandmother. She was affectionate and fun and always smelled like cookies. As she baked and worked around the house, she sang songs about God and this man called Jesus. She taught me the words to the song, "Jesus loves me," so I knew he loved me, too.

One morning, my mother told me my grandparents were taking me to church. I was thrilled because I thought that's where God lived, and it must be a truly grand place. Dressed in my white smocked dress, white patent-leather Mary Jane shoes, and lacy socks, I couldn't wait for my grandparents' car to arrive in the driveway.

I had seen the big stone church before, but I had never been inside. The stained glass windows reflected rainbows of color throughout the sanctuary, and the sound of singing was heavenly. I was practically dancing on my tip-toes with anticipation. When the singing stopped, a tall, dignified man rose slowly from a high-back chair on the stage. He raised a tattered black book high in the air. After a poignant moment of silence, he sternly spoke.

"This is the Good Book—the book of right and wrong, good and bad. And *you* better choose the right way."

He bowed his head and earnestly pleaded with God to keep "his flock" from sin. He beseeched Jesus to cover us with His blood and save us all from hellfire. I was confused about the sheep and more than a little concerned about the blood when suddenly this man slammed his hand down on the lectern so loudly that it startled me.

He spoke in a thunderous voice, and what I heard frightened this little girl terribly. His message was simple: God hates filth, and when we sin, we become filthy rags that disgust Him. He warned us that if we didn't stop sinning, God would throw us into the fire where we would burn alive forever.

Shaking, I huddled as close to my grandmother as possible. The man spoke with such authority; no one could doubt a word he said. Grandma Susie, observing my nervousness after church, explained that being a filthy rag was okay, because, "When you›re good, God forgives your sins."

Her explanation didn't make me feel better, because she didn't seem to know that I was a bad little girl. My mother constantly reminded me that I was a bad child, and that I had made her life miserable. She wanted me out of her sight. No matter how hard I tried, I couldn't make her happy. I felt bad to the bone. And now, even worse, I had a new name for myself: I was a sinner, destined for hell.

Even though I never went back to my grandparents' church, my relatives told me enough about sin so I knew I'd better pray hard for this filthy girl to be forgiven. I prayed from guilt and from fear, earnestly bargaining with God nightly: "If you forgive me for what I have done up to now, I'll never do it again." And I meant it wholeheartedly.

The following day, despite my promise to God, I would do something that made my mother furious. She would tell me again, "You're driving me crazy!" It seemed clear I was never going to be acceptable to my mother and probably not to God, either. *I must be such a disappointment to them both.* Despite my best efforts, I kept on sinning and wanted to give up. But how does a five-year-old escape this kind of nightmare?

Over the years, I tried to go back to church. Every time, it seemed something worse happened. The disappointments and condemnation I felt from the church added to my sense of hopelessness. By the time I was a teenager, I had run as far from God, the church, and my life as possible. To end my failures, I tried to take my life.

I was on the last gasp of ever trying again.

The treatment center's solution was to turn to this God, who seemed full of empty promises. He'd never answered any of my prayers! If I went back to the church here, I knew I'd hear the same load of bull.

But… what if they were right? No, I couldn't, wouldn't even consider it, because there was no way to get there from here. The staff told me I couldn't have the life I wanted if I wouldn't take Step One and admit I was powerless. It was easy to admit I'd made a mess of my life, but I couldn't bear to think I had no power at all. That would have been as terrifying as the helplessness I felt as a child. Surely, if I could read the right book—or find the right therapist, guru, exercise plan, relationship, or medication—it would finally prove to be the help I needed. Yes, I needed help—but not from their God.

While the other "inmates" (my name for us) seemed to be getting happier day by day, laughing and joking, I was pouting and balking. They told each other they were getting down on their knees every morning to tell God they needed his help. Then they prayed specific prayers from the "Big Book," to set up a hopeful expectancy for their day. I thought, *No way.* Yet they seemed to be changing, while I felt stuck.

No great spiritual revelation made me decide to get on my knees. Still, as I ran through the long list of all the other things I had been willing to try—weird diets, fasting, dancing, meditation, twisting myself into yoga positions, living in an ashram, and hundreds of hours of all kinds of therapies—I thought, *What do I have to lose? I've been halfway around the world seeking answers. And here is a method I haven't tried. If this is working for them, might it work for me?*

Reluctantly and skeptically, I decided to perform this charade.

I was so embarrassed to be seen on my knees talking out loud to someone I didn't believe was there, I went into the large, walk-in clothes closet and closed the door. Feeling foolish and fake, I repeated the words they gave me to say. For more than four weeks, I performed this ritual every morning, noticing no change.

On the thirty-third day as a patient in a treatment facility, I got down on my knees and said the exact words I had recited every morning: *God, I am powerless.* When the words left my mouth, a wave of sweet relief washed over me and took my angst and struggle out to a sea of forgetfulness.

Inhaling deeply, I looked around. Nothing had changed in the space, but something had changed in me. My mind was still. My heart was calm and full. Contentment wrapped around me like a warm blanket. I felt whole, like I had everything I had ever longed for in that moment. I wanted to stay in that closet and hold onto the feeling forever.

Had I remembered anything from the days of my Bible-reading youth, I would surely have recognized that the Lord promised, "I will never leave you or forsake you" (Joshua 1:5).

Had God shown up in the closet? Was it God holding me?

It was an unexpected relief to realize I was powerless and I didn't have to depend solely on my own resolve. For years, I'd tried to reassure myself, but I didn't have the reassurance to give.

One week after that sweet morning in the closet, the staff said I was ready for release. I had reluctantly been in this facility for forty days, pushing back against their every suggestion and rule—but now, I didn't want to leave. I had run from God for thirty years, never knowing He went with me to every place I ran. Although I had given up on Him, He never gave up on me.

Had I found a miracle? Maybe the miracle found me.

As I exited the treatment center, a sign on the inside wall declared: "You are a miracle."

Covid Miracles
by Bonnie McLean

The blessings that have come from Covid
vastly outweigh the miseries.

One morning, I awoke feeling very fatigued and thought, "I must be working harder than I realize." After two cups of coffee, I went on with my day. By evening, I felt more fatigued, so I went to bed and remained there—for a week. Much of that week has escaped my memory, except eating a slice of watermelon, sipping some water, and calling my nurse practitioner. She advised me to go to a hospital emergency room if my symptoms got worse.

A friend of mine who was experiencing the same symptoms was convinced we had the stomach flu. It was my hope that was the case, but I still got tested for Covid. I never received the results. The health department left a few telephone messages asking me to return their call, but calling them back led me to an answering machine that didn't take messages. I gave up.

During that week, I had no cough and no sore throat or fever. All I wanted to do was sleep.

By the end of the week, I felt even more fatigued, with body aches and shooting pains in my head. Although I decided to take my nurse practitioner's advice and go to the emergency room, my mind was foggy, and I didn't think to call a friend or neighbor. Instead, I called a taxi. The driver looked nervous when I staggered out of my house and asked to be taken to the nearest emergency room.

Upon my arrival, someone immediately put me in a bed. My blood pressure was 70/40. My pulse was weak and fast, yet I still had no fever. The nurse asked how I had managed to walk in.

My test for Covid-19 was positive, and I was admitted.

This was the first day of my two-week hospital stay. As with the first week at home, I don't remember much except my overwhelming desire for constant sleep. However, I do remember my TV was tuned to a nature show the hospital ran twenty-four hours a day. I went to sleep and woke up watching scenes of waterfalls, mountains, and wild animals from all over the world. Every day, I looked forward to seeing these beautiful and peaceful nature scenes.

I also remember taking many medications, including a blood thinner, an anti-inflammatory, a diuretic, an antibiotic, and melatonin at night. My doctors also gave me Vitamin C, Vitamin D3, and zinc, and I was grateful they were willing to provide me with the anti-viral drug remdesivir and convalescent plasma from someone who had recovered from Covid and still had antibodies.

These last two experimental therapies, which were administered by IV, probably contributed to saving my life. The skill of the nurses who had to start my IVs was impressive, because my veins seemed to disappear from the frequent lab work. Having spent twenty years as an RN, I know how challenging finding a vein can be.

One memory that stands out in my mind is of a nurse's aide who stopped what he was doing, looked me straight in the eye, and said, "This virus wants to kill you. The way it does it is to make you want to sleep... not move... not breathe. You have to make yourself breathe deeply and move as much as you can." Chris Cuomo had said the same thing on TV when he had Covid. It was hard work to remember to make myself move and breathe, but doing so made a difference.

All Covid patients were in isolation, which meant no visitors.

During my hospital stay, I was moved to six different rooms. There were so many Covid patients admitted for treatment that the hospital opened new areas to accommodate us all. Thank goodness, a friend of mine offered to be my patient advocate. That was a godsend. She stayed in touch with me, the front desk, and my family and close friends.

Staff did not come into our rooms unless it was absolutely necessary. Many of the nurses were brought in from other units of the hospital. Two of my nurses had had Covid themselves. They both said that, even though they had tested negative and had been cleared to return to work, they still experienced a lot of fatigue and just didn't feel completely back to normal.

One reason Covid is so dangerous is the virus initially evades detection by the body's immune system. By the time Covid is recognized, it has embedded itself in the vital organs, especially the lungs, where it often causes pneumonia. Eventually, I developed a cough, difficulty breathing, and a fever. I was on oxygen, but it didn't feel like my body was getting enough, so I thought something was wrong with my oxygen equipment.

It took four hours for the front desk to have a respiratory therapist check the equipment, even with my advocate's intervention. By then, I was crying and my whole body was shaking. I don't know what my vital signs were, but I was whisked to the intensive care unit and placed on 50 percent oxygen.

I vaguely remember going into a peaceful place within myself. Despite being alone much of the time, I didn't feel alone—I felt part of something so much bigger than me. Even though I didn't have the classical near-death experience that so many patients describe, this felt like I could have easily left my body to go into a beautiful, loving place. While in that place, I was aware of many prayers coming my way... from my family, friends, and loved ones, and also from patients and people I didn't even know.

One of my patients, I learned later, had called a nunnery and asked them to add me to their prayers. I realized I didn't want to leave these people. The prayers awakened a desire to stay in my body... in my life.

Two days later, I was moved out of the ICU and back out into a regular room. In less than a week, I was discharged with oxygen, a bedside commode, and a walker. It still took several more weeks for me to recover and regain my strength, and then several more for me to test negative and return to work.

I returned home a changed person.

Having Covid was a miserable experience... the most miserable experience in my life! I don't wish it on anyone. But the blessings that have come from Covid vastly outweigh the miseries. Because of the experience, I feel a deep gratitude for so many things I had previously taken for granted.

I'm grateful for all the people who helped me, including the doctors and essential workers who are saving lives like mine every day. First responders and essential workers are my heroes. My gratitude extended to my family and friends, my patient advocate, and all the people who prayed for me. My spiritual community collected money to help with the hospital expenses during the time I was not able to work, and my gratitude includes them. I'm grateful to my boyfriend, who drove an hour and a half twice a day for two weeks to check my house and take care of my cats.

For years, I'd looked for a community to live in with like-minded and like-hearted people. This experience helped me realize I was already a part of the community I had been searching for.

I have always believed in prayer as well as angels. My Covid experience turned my belief into a deep knowing of their power. I continue to feel deep gratitude when I wake up in the morning and have energy to live my daily life, to love the people in it and to feel the love in return, and to be able to appreciate the beauty of nature.

I believe that miracles can be like the ripples in a pond.

One of the most beautiful miracles of my experience with Covid had to do with the young man who told me to move and breathe while I was hospitalized. After being interviewed about my experience with Covid by a local radio station, I received a message on Facebook from his girlfriend. She wanted me to know that he had heard the interview while he was driving, and had called and told her how deeply touched he was by my mentioning how much he had helped me.

Miracles expand to touch more than one person. Allowing one of our healthcare professionals to know the importance of what they do, especially during this pandemic, makes me feel that the blessings of my experience with Covid were able to come full circle.

An Intimate Journey with Exhaustion
by Tamara Knox

Walk slow, talk slow, breath slow, be slow.

I was headed down a dark road and my life was anything but balanced. Thankfully, my body decided to slow me down and communicate to me that something was drastically wrong. The pain and weakness I was experiencing demanded an intervention.

Stress, heartbreak, illness, and loss were all too common to me.

It had been a rough few years and a debilitating summer. Although I had the will to go on, my internal system was failing. My weight had dropped, my digestion was compromised, and my strength was near zero. The happy smile on my face was no match for the dwindling light inside by body. Each day, I was getting weaker, and I had very few answers on how to get better.

My nervous system was taxed, and I felt every ounce of burnout one could feel. To cook and clean was difficult, as was engaging in conversation and relationships. On edge and exhausted, I called out for help, saying, "Spirit, hold me, love me, guide me. Show me what needs to heal." My prayer was sincere. I was desperate and needed the Divine.

In an instant, I knew I had connected to the energetics of something powerful. Any cry for help usually awakens deep parts of one's soul. Inside my body, I felt and heard a hum, and my cells began to orchestrate something sacred—just as if they had been waiting for me to ask. A resonance called Oneness reminded me that everything would be okay. With this awareness came a peacefulness I hadn't felt in years. This peacefulness bypassed all sensations of my body and provided a disconnect from the mind. I became infinite space with passive breath to the void.

My feelings and emotions were at ease, and in turn, this dominated over all other sensations. This new feeling and inner awareness were informative—a "forever" imprint to turn to when in need. At that moment, I chose it, honored it, and became it.

Later that night, when all got quiet, I was able to revisit the precious moments of the day. A part of me wanted to analyze it all, but within a sudden breath, I heard the words of Spirit lovingly whisper, "Eat, sleep, and move." Not exactly sure what that meant, my curiosity led me to stay alert. *Move*, I thought. *Hmmm... exercise? How am I supposed to exercise when I'm exhausted, in pain, and underweight?*

I stayed quiet, deeply connected to myself, as if Spirit knew I was confused.

Squeeze the qi/chi.

With this message, Divine insight began. The guidance of "squeeze the chi" was the initiating of a new movement for me. I was familiar with tai chi and qi gong and had previously studied dance and other forms of movement, but this was unlike any other movement and proved the most profound to my exhausted, immobile body.

That night, a movement meditation began which became the core practice and foundation for having the strength to breathe deeply, get out of bed, and regain some quality of life. This practice was a gift as I began to address the pain, overwhelm, exhaustion, and regeneration on all levels; mentally, physically, emotionally, and spiritually. It allowed me to seek a quiet place internally and to recalibrate with the demands of life and subtle energies within.

Shaky from being so tired, I lay down. As my head hit the pillow, my body settled into a cradle position with the covers adding the needed comfort for my sensitive nervous system and skin. As I put one hand on my chest and the other on my belly and began to breathe, the voice of a loved one from the other side offered advice. As always, I had a notebook close by—a necessity for remembering and deciphering supreme guidance. They stated and I wrote:

Lie down. Feel your body. Feel the places of exhaustion and tightness. Breathe gently for a few minutes and allow places to settle. Be open to change. Allow the pain and allow the comfort with no judgement of either. Allow yourself to feel the tired, stressed spaces. Allow yourself to feel lightness and spaces of flow. Then, slightly tense your body. Tense all of it or just a part of it. Even a fist is fine. How one moves and connects with their body and breath is their own intimate dance. Enjoy.

My first experience was profound, and all I did was squeeze my fists. Feeling so weak and tired, I could not have done much more. After squeezing my fists gently about ten times, they decided to move on their own, flexing and making small circles. My hands and fingers found their own rhythm. In that time, I felt more energy within as I was creating space for blood and lymph to move. My blood vessels constricted and relaxed. Each day, I practiced with a new part of the body: legs, fingers, toes, hips, neck, eyes. All small movements and very delicate to start.

As the movements became a routine, adding sound and breath advanced the practice to a new level. The breath was slow, gentle, and delicate, along with the sound. Any sound that vibrated well in the moment was perfect for healing. Even a light hum became powerful. My most invigorating sounds, although whispers, were and still are *swoosh, mmm, hmmm, ooo, eee* and *pah*. I quickly understood it was not just about making the sound, but allowing, enjoying, and being one with it.

Sound was now deemed as sacred. I had a new passion, and my ears were on high alert for any new frequency that wanted to speak and calibrate my internal foundation. I noticed that, although each practice was different, finding the similarities built a base that led to moments beyond belief; magical, regenerative, and pain-free moments.

To bypass exhaustion and pain, I had to get quiet and listen to the subtleties within. As I connected, I realized the smallest pulse of breath, sound, or movement would allow for a cascade of information from the void to penetrate within. It was a communication that calls for consciousness to bathe one in the elixir of self-intimacy and vast oneness. It was refreshing to discover this inner essence by gently moving and exploring infinite new spaces.

The practice allowed my body to recalibrate in a way where movement became possible without extreme pain and shortness of breath. Daily tasks that had been nearly impossible, like pushing the vacuum, soon became enjoyable and rewarding. I was able to appreciate this new connection to my body and value the wisdom and healing that came along with it.

Continuously getting quiet altered my nervous system to help me move chi, strengthen the mitochondria, and recalibrate my depleted immune system. With daily commitment, food allergies started to disappear, my mental focus became better, and I had much more resilience for unexpected stressors that came my way. The practice was cumulative; when I did it every day for at least three to five minutes, I saw momentary change that led to greater gains and personal satisfaction. Sinus pressure, tension headaches, shallow breath, allergies, and joint and back pain—all players of chronic inflammation—responded well to this process.

To restore this balance gave me an intimate connection to flow and peace.

This practice started out as movement and then deepened into the thought and initiation of the movement: the micro moments of micromovements that reflected deep awareness of universal energy and its essence. I was able to see in the stillness and became aware that this space was redefining my existence. A deep change was happening as I was letting go of identity, grief, the past, and resistance of both body and mind, allowing a new identity of light. I became the awareness of presence and love, beyond the body and mind, in an initiation to pure intimacy.

My journey with exhaustion gave me the insight to begin to receive the deepest communication with Spirit and energy. I am grateful to have had this experience for without it, true healing could not have been possible. To be in deep connection with one's own body and space is powerful and initiates one of the most profound aspects of human evolution. To me, evolution is a process of nature, while *conscious evolution* is a relationship with nature and beyond. When I'm in a deep relationship with the intimacies of life, I can bypass trauma, pain, hardship, and exhaustion, to become fulfilled and well-balanced.

Life is a miracle. Consciousness allows for exploration and experience of this. I realized the miracle for me was to see where my restrictive thinking and behaviors were affecting my movement and how my physical resistance kept me from changing and working through life's complexities in a healthy way. The miracle was letting go of who I thought I was.

In the practice, I was able to be my true essence—not my mind, my pain or exhaustion, or my past. I wasn't the memory of my pain, which was the biggest fear and discomfort. I was *awareness* at its core. I went from being in pain and exhaustion to Being. By connecting deeply with my spirit, I was able to transcend mental and physical limitations and become more than the ailment or dis-ease.

This awareness has led me to a continuous journey of self-respect and self-love.

The Un-birthday Gift
by Myriam Ben Salem

A gift engraved in your heart for a lifetime.

During my childhood, all that mattered was to be perfect. Developmentally, I performed earlier than the average child; walking, talking, singing, acting, dancing—you name it. Although I was highly praised by others, my true feelings were rarely seen, heard, or understood. Attunement parenting was not my reality. I rarely felt worthy of having needs and even less worthy of having those needs met.

Inevitably, it became evident that I was an unaware empath and top performer suffering from Impostor-Syndrome, which refers to my internal experience of believing I am not as competent as others perceive. Despite being adored by my teachers and my parents' friends, and continuously celebrated for my achievements, I dove into life with negative self-esteem.

Between pleasing and achieving, I had zero access to the psychological air needed to thrive. Because of my caregivers' unhealthy bond, I had to develop hypervigilance and lofty human behavior and observation levels. As a result, I became an expert in spotting any microscopic swing in someone's mood and responding accordingly. Simultaneously, and because I never suspected this skill to be part of my survival strategy, I expected others to read my mind as well. As a result, my relationships suffered.

It was a delusional existence nourished by affirmations.

Despite having enjoyed a brief break from work to start a self-improvement journey, my existence was still meaningless to me. I didn't learn to respect and enjoy myself and merely created a fragile balance. Initially, the journey resulted in elevating my self-esteem, bolstering my imagined confidence, visualizing some motivational financial abundance, and creating an overall better personal feeling. It was a fabulous practice—until it wasn't anymore.

Two significant parallel incidents occurred at this time that fueled my ingrained limiting beliefs and overrode my affirmations: a problem with my employer and a breakup with my ex-boyfriend, who I sincerely believed was the love of my life. Disoriented, I decided to give up on everything and go back to my home country of Tunisia.

Instead of starting a new, serious inner-discovery journey, I immersed myself in studying a business idea and numbed my immense sorrow through any distraction, guaranteeing "highs" that allowed me to feel a little better about myself. One of my great loves was going to a cozy co-working space. Unfortunately—or maybe, fortunately—a malignant narcissist, or what some experts designate as a "sadistic psychopath," profiled me.

Guilty as charged.

I admit to making his mission easier. As a quality of an unaware, passionate empath, it was not unusual for me to cry publicly. My narcissist took advantage of one of my crying episodes by handing me a tissue. He was limitlessly charming. He told me he could relate and made me believe he was a crier, too. He was convincing, to say the least. He studied what set my soul on fire and quickly gathered as much data as possible so he could effortlessly mirror my emotions.

Curiously, my gut-instinct told me something was off every time we met. His toxic energy made me uneasy. Sadly, my many limiting beliefs caused my intuition to be anything but unfiltered and pure. Self-doubt and loathing were much easier to believe. When he was courting me, during the early days, I made the mistake of ridiculing him. It was an example of how I used to be "an idiot trying to prove her self-confidence" in a messy way.

I had never witnessed anything crueler than his revenge.

After a first love-bombing period, the devaluation phase began. It was exceedingly subtle. He knew I was in the middle of an existential crisis. His brilliant attempt to deceive me into questioning my perception of reality—known as "gaslighting"—had fertile ground. It didn't take him more than three months to destroy my self-esteem entirely. I was left in the darkest of places and decided to radically stop my suffering in September 2018.

At the last moment, as I made plans to end my life, I was spared by the grace of my pure love divinity through an out-of-body experience. It was as if the servant-leader in me dissociated from myself to help me see my unhealthy ego's lies and realize that this gigantic universe does not revolve around my small self.

My move to end my life became the beginning of my rebirth. Most importantly, during this supernatural dissociation, I could visualize how my purpose on this planet was to carry out a mission that goes beyond me, to be a Universal Citizen who would unapologetically contribute—through my voice and model servant leadership—to create our beautiful "World of Pandora," a world where all living creatures would be interconnected and life would be honored and lived to its fullest.

That was the moment of my migration from being religious to spiritual.

The butterfly within me took time to emerge. First, the caterpillar had to heal deep wounds and gain strength to start the most rewarding investment of its whole existence: destroying all my limiting beliefs, both about myself and the world.

At the beginning of 2019, I sustained an unpleasant accident; it affected my patella. The accident was devastating because exercise was among my foremost healing resources. I stopped for a moment and reflected thereon. What if this was the universe telling me I was ready for my significant homework?

Listening, I rewired the invasive subconscious program never written by me in the first place to align with the primary center and natural compass the creator granted us at birth; the unchangeable and timeless principles of life. My gratitude to the universe for the trauma that led me to this discovery is beyond description. It was what I needed to wake up.

Throughout this process, my pain was almost unbearable. I doubted it, detested it, felt absurd, and wanted to give up more times than I can remember. But there was a secret to my win: thanks to my drive for transformation, I persisted. Every time I was willing to give up, all I needed to do was remember I was doing it *for the world*. In those moments, my bravery grew.

It took almost seven months to rewrite most of my inner program. My close friends know I repeatedly express my gratitude for my trauma. Every incident was necessary for me at the time it took place.

In order to confirm my doubt about a person in my close circle, I followed some mental health training and discovered an unpleasant truth. Chaos had triggered my "savior" pattern; the comic part was that I unconsciously rejected its existence. To me, this is the most incredible thing about the subconscious program.

No matter how many algorithms I could've rewritten or the level of my reconnection with the true self before the conditioning started, there will unavoidably be some unsuspected patterns I'll discover as new events take place in my life without my permission.

Even more mind-blowing is that yielding my rescuer pattern has been more challenging than the whole program-rewriting process. It's been nine months, and it's still a work in progress for me. The resistance is fierce, to say the least.

One impressive detail is how many layers I've found. What helps me move forward is my noble purpose. Unlike the limiting beliefs I consider bad, being a "savior" is intrinsically good.

For the first time in thirty-six years on earth, I decided not to celebrate my birthday.

A few days before my birthday, I published a post on one of my social media platforms. It was in French, because many of my connections don't understand English, our third language. I officially announced my decision not to celebrate my birthday anymore; instead, I'd replace it with my re-birthday.

The number of reactions I had the honor to receive, most of which were private, exceeded all my expectations. I could barely believe how deeply my proclamation resonated with so many individuals. Many responded using the words *courage* and *strength of character*.

I might have decided not to celebrate my birth, but the universe had bigger plans for me. While in my favorite co-working space, I received a call from my beloved Swedish friend, with whom I only have real talks. We chatted for about twenty minutes.

A girl seated close to me prepared to leave. On her way out, she stopped by me and, with anguished eyes and a trembling voice, said, "I rarely take the initiative to talk to strangers, but I couldn't help it today. You impacted my spirit in a way I can't even describe. I apologize for unintentionally hearing your conversation. I'm going through some hard times. Hearing you talk about your challenges with such resilience, and expressing such unbelievable gratitude because it happened when you were ready to handle it—as well as your faith that everything is going to be okay—was beyond inspiring!"

She moved me to my core. I gave her one of my warmest hugs before wishing her peace and saying goodbye. It was by far the most adorable gift of my thirty-six years, an un-birthday gift money can't buy. This joyous culmination of all my challenges, lessons, and reprogramming will be engraved in my heart for a lifetime.

Final Thoughts

The stories in this section showed us that we have a world of wealth when we have our health. Many of the authors, like Peggy Willms and Mary Ellen Lucas, trusted in their Higher Power and believed that everything would be alright. Dr. Anne Worth's disdain for her treatment center turned into faith in herself, out of which grew hope for a better future. In each case, the mayhem of stones thrown into the waters of life became rings of hope that connected people to more positive outcomes. As Bonnie McLean so aptly wrote, "Miracles expand to touch more than one person."

PART 3

GRIEF AND LOSS
Let the Circle Be Unbroken

The connections are real.
The signs and messages are all around us.

Bonfire Fire of the Vanities!

by Kathleen O'Keefe-Kanavos

There is no doubt in my mind that synchronicities and Divine Intervention were at play in this story.

The desperate cell phone buzzing becomes part of a dream that leads me up the rabbit hole of sleep and into my waking world in Florida. Loki and Cleopatra, my Siamese cats, howl their muffled displeasure at being disturbed from beneath the comforter at five a.m. in January. *Who on earth would call me at this ungodly hour? I wondered. Everyone knows not to call me in the morning!*

It's Julie's number, my next-door neighbor in California. My husband Peter is in California.

Something is wrong. My hair begins to stand on end.

"Hello?" I croak.

"Kat, the condo just burned down!" the breathless male voice says from Julie's phone. It takes me a minute to recognize the voice is Peter's and that he is referring to our condo.

"Your new Mercedes just blew up in the garage. The fire department is here, so I'll call you back later. My phone is in the bedroom, and I can't get to it because of the smoke and flames, so I'll call you from someone else's phone. If you see an unknown number, just answer it. Go back to sleep."

"Wait! Are you okay?" The wail of firetrucks amid the mayhem becomes louder until I can barely hear him.

"Yeah! But it's freezing out here in the desert this early in the morning, and I only have on my PJ bottoms," he yells. "No shoes or shirt. Gotta go! Call ya' later."

Holy Crap! How the hell was I supposed to go back to sleep after that news? My new car blew up? What about all my stuff? My clothes, shoes, pictures of my deceased parents on their wedding day, my mask collection from around the world for my Dream Therapy classes. MY LIBRARY!

Focus on that later, my inner voice says. *Help Peter now.*

I immediately call all our friends in the Country Club and tell them what happened, and that Peter is running around outside in the cold with no clothing or phone. Thank goodness my friends answer their phones early in the morning. Then I call Julie back to be sure she is okay and to find out what happened.

"Peter ran over here to my house at around two a.m. and started beating on the door to wake me up so I could move my car out of the garage, so it wouldn't catch on fire, too. Then he ran around on bare feet and banged on everyone else's doors to wake them up. There are huge firetrucks here blocking the road. Can you hear them? Oh shit, Kat! Your roof just fell in. Flames are coming out the bedroom windows and through the hole in the roof… and there's a whole bunch of golf carts heading across the golf course, beeping their horns and flashing their lights."

The flotilla of golf carts were friends coming to Peter's rescue with shoes, shirts, and a jacket. God bless them!

The worst part of the whole ordeal was waiting to hear back from Peter.

Waiting in the dark, while hugging my cats, gave me time to reflect on the situation… and it frightened the crap out of me so badly I began to shiver. Our original plan had been to go to California together with the cats and stay for a couple of months and then return to Florida. I was really looking forward to seeing my friends again. The day before we were to leave for the airport, I suddenly decided not to go… just changed my mind. I wasn't sure why I didn't want to go anymore, but my desire to remain in Florida was so strong. I attributed it to the fact that things were still closed in California due to COVID. There would be no parties, playing tennis, or going out to dinner with friends. So why bother making the long plane ride across the country with two drugged pets?

"Honey, I'm going to stay here with the cats. You go check on the house. I'll drive you to the airport," I had told Peter two days earlier.

I believe the sudden decision to stay in Florida saved my life.

"So according to the fire department's preliminary damage report, the fire started in the garage," Peter told me a short time later. "It was either your car, the golf cart, or the instant hot water-heater, because there is nothing else in there to catch fire or start a fire. If I hadn't had jet lag-related insomnia and been in the living room watching TV at two a.m.,

I would have been asleep in the bedroom, which shares a wall with the garage, when your car exploded. If the smoke hadn't killed me in my sleep, I wouldn't have made it out of the room alive because we have those gratings on the windows to keep stray golf balls from breaking the glass. It would have been impossible to get them off with all the smoke in the room. Our bedroom is a total loss. It's also a death trap. We need to rethink those gratings."

"If you were in the living room, how did you know there was a fire?" I ask.

"The fire alarms went off in the house, but I thought the batteries needed replacing. Then there was a bang, and thought we were having an earthquake until I smelled smoke and went to investigate. Black smoke was pouring through the top and bottom of the garage door. So, without thinking, I opened the door to see what was going on. A huge ball of fire chased me down the hallway, out the kitchen door, and onto the golf course. Then I started banging on the neighbors' doors to wake them up. They looked pretty confused when they saw me standing there with singed hair and no shirt, shoes, or phone. Someone called the fire department. If you had been asleep in the bedroom, Kat... I think I would have lost you... and definitely the cats. It was a miracle you didn't come."

"The important thing is, you're okay. We only lost unimportant stuff," I say. "Stuff we collected for our vanity, like clothes we never even wore. They probably still had the price tags hanging on them."

Suddenly, pictures of things collected from all over the world as an Army-brat flash in my mind's eye. I remember the hand-made Christmas tree ornaments my parents began collecting on my first birthday. My silk bedding; the sterling silver flatware handed down by my parents;

ornate table linens from summers spent in Italy. My collection of antique crystal. All toast now. But I wasn't going to say that to my husband.

"Yeah, but we lost *a lot* of stuff, Kat. And every time I close my eyes, I see and feel that huge fireball!"

In the days that followed, I reflected on those losses.

Yes, we lost all our stuff—but it could have been so much worse. We could have lost each other in the flames, along with our neighbors. And it is very likely we would have lost Loki and Cleopatra.

The bottom line is, we only lost collected stuff—just vanity stuff— and most of that can be replaced… or not. People, pets, and loved ones cannot be replaced. And true friends are priceless.

You don't know who your true friends are until they come barreling across the golf course *toward* the fire, rather than running away from it, in the dark of the night to help you out with shoes.

Another miracle was Peter's phone and wallet.

When the firemen entered our bedroom, which was reduced to ash and soot, Peter's phone and wallet were still on the scorched nightstand, untouched by the fire. They felt a bit warm but not burned or melted when the fireman handed them to Peter.

It would have been difficult to replace all the credit cards, medical cards, and other things stuffed in his wallet during the best of times, but this was during COVID. Thankfully, nothing needed to be replaced. It was as if the angels had reached down through the flames, cradled his wallet and phone in their hands, and said, "Not this stuff!"

Our friends rose to the occasion. One offered their rental condo to Peter, which was a few doors down from our condo. We'll rent there while we rebuild. Another loaned him their extra vehicle until his car gets cleaned. And everyone brought him food, some of which was from our freezers.

When the condo's power was cut, I made another frantic call to my friends and begged them to go into the condo as soon as it was safe and clean out all the food in the freezers—filet mignon, lobster tails, shrimp—and they gladly obliged. Then they cooked much of it up for Peter.

There is no doubt in my mind that synchronicities and Divine Intervention were at play in this story.

If Peter had not had jet lag, he would have been asleep in the death-trap bedroom. If I had not changed my mind at the last minute, I would have been asleep in the bedroom with Peter and the cats. Despite a devastating fire in the middle of the night while most neighbors slept, no lives were lost, only stuff.

I believe that at some time in the past year, I must have looked into my bulging closets and said, "Oh God, I need a miracle to help me clean this stuff out."

Boom—done! A bonfire of the vanities. God's always listening. Another miracle!

A Little Glimpse of Heaven

Teresa Velardi

I caught a glimpse of it in my dying mother's eyes. A miracle!

Mom's time on this earth was coming to an end. After years of treatment for lung cancer, she was tired of the mayhem of so many doctors, hospitalizations, and chemotherapy treatments and was ready to leave this world.

Her journey was not comfortable or easy, but her faith was immense and unwavering. Mom rarely complained throughout her treatment, even though she endured many surgical procedures, including brain surgery when her cancer metastasized there.

There was always hope from the next surgery, the newest medical breakthrough or experimental treatment. But the day I took her for a consult with yet another doctor who said he might be able to stop the spread to her spine and ultimately her spinal fluid with a procedure called an *ablation*, I saw the look in her eyes that said, "I'm tired. I don't want to do this anymore."

I thanked the doctor for his time while my cousin, who had gone with us to the appointment, continued to ask procedural questions in hopes of getting the piece of information that would change Mom's mind. Once again, I expressed my gratitude for the doctor's time and told my cousin it was time to leave. Then I wheeled Mom out of the exam room and headed for the elevator to take her home.

There would be no more treatment.

Mom was comfortable with her decision, and so was I. She had met every challenge with grace. My siblings, on the other hand—well, for a while, that was mayhem. It amazes me how much insanity can rise to the surface when the fear of losing a loved one is before you.

As things progressed and Mom needed more care, I took three days off from my job and headed to my childhood home to set up the hospice program and to make sure Mom was well cared for by family members who lived close by. I planned to return to work to get the paperwork done for family medical leave and then head back to Mom's to spend the last days she would have on Earth with her.

Mom was a woman who thoroughly enjoyed her life.

When I got to her house, she talked about going to the casino in Connecticut one more time. My cousin, who was living there, had "promised" her he would take her. The nurse who came to the house that day said it was ill-advised to take her anywhere, as she had a bladder infection and would be extremely uncomfortable making the three-hour drive. She reluctantly agreed to stay home. That didn't stop her from winning our money when a bunch of us played cards with her after dinner. She was so lucky!

When Mom had a feeling she was going to win money, she'd rally a friend or two together to go to a local bingo game, the casino, or jai alai, and she would always win! Las Vegas was one of her favorite places, and if you guessed that she was a winner there, you are correct. She came home with extra cash every time.

She was filled with joy and had many friends, including some she'd known for more than fifty years. She was always surrounded by people who loved her dearly. She was my best friend.

I spent a lot of time talking with Mom.

During the next couple of days, besides putting together the hospice care and making sure she had what she needed, I was by her side. Most of the time, it was just the two of us. She would be in her recliner, watching TV behind closed eyelids or reminiscing out loud.

My father had passed away ten years prior, and although she would talk about him sometimes, she was strolling down memory lane more than usual during those last few days. I knew Dad was near and he would be part of the welcoming party when her time came.

While we were talking one afternoon, I asked, "How are you doing, Mom? Do you need anything?"

I wasn't expecting her to say, "I'm tired, Teresa. It's almost time for me to go. I know where I'm going, and I'm ready. I'm sure going to miss you, though."

With tears in my eyes, I assured her that she would always be in my heart and that I would see her again someday. My faith allowed me to be confident in that statement. I know in my heart that's true.

During this time, my sister-in-law had undergone major surgery and was in a hospital in upstate NY. My brother and my niece were doing their best to convince the doctor to release her so she could make the five-hour trip to Long Island to say her goodbye to Mom. The doctor finally agreed. If she was stable enough the following afternoon, he would release her to make the trip.

With about forty hours to go before she saw them, Mom wasn't doing well. She spent most of the day in bed and kept telling me the names of people she wanted to see—the doctor who had taken care of her for so many years, and several friends and family members. I made the calls, and she got to see most of them that day.

That night, while I was tucking her in and talking about her day, she got completely distracted from the conversation. She kept looking over my shoulder to the corner of the room where it met the ceiling. Although I tried to get her attention, her eyes were fixed on that spot. Soon, she began to giggle. I watched her for a few more minutes before asking her, "Mom, what's going on?"

Then it hit me. "Okay, Mom, who's here?"

She turned and looked at me. One-by-one, she said the names of all my deceased relatives. As I listened, I saw her face light up with joy.

"Mom, what are they doing?" I asked.

"They're cooking the pasta for the party," she said, "I'm going home." Her joy and excitement were palpable!

I had heard of people having similar experiences of seeing their deceased relatives before making the journey to heaven, but I caught a glimpse of it in my dying mother's eyes. A miracle!

She slept peacefully through the night.

The next morning, we got the call that my brother and his family were on their way. Mom was in bed the entire day, drifting in and out of consciousness. The hospice nurses stopped by, medicating her and making sure she was comfortable. Family members came and went.

About dinner time, my brother and his family arrived. When I told her, she immediately opened her eyes wide and said, "Get me up! I want to get up!"

My aunt is a nurse; she and I got Mom up, changed, and into the wheelchair. When we wheeled her into the kitchen, she was a whole new woman. She ate dinner; she laughed and was silly with her great-grandchildren, thoroughly enjoying time with everyone. She even played cards! Go figure. If you had told me a few hours earlier that this would be the scenario, I'd have told you, "You're out of your mind!"

But there she was, fully awake, aware, and alive. Another miracle!

When we put her to bed that night, I prayed that she would be able to greet the last couple of people who were coming to see her the next day. I knew how much she wanted to see her doctor.

Mom spent the next day in the bed, in and out of consciousness again, hospice nurses overseeing her care and friends and family by her side. About midday, the doorbell rang. Doctor B. had arrived, and I knew Mom would be so happy!

We went to her room, where my sister and nieces were around her. They kept trying to wake her. No luck. The river of tears began among them.

I went over and took my mother by the hands and shouted, "Ma!" She turned her head to me, looked me in the eyes, and said, "What?"

My sister's jaw dropped.

"Doctor B is here."

Mom's face lit up. This was the final person on her list of people to see before she went home. I propped her up a bit. I listened to her thank the doctor for all she had done for her. Doctor B. had given and arranged for

117

my mother's best care while she fought the horror called cancer. Mom was and still is the most courageous woman I've ever known. Even when she could have taken her very last breath, she was able to articulate her gratitude.

We could hear her breathing was labored as Doctor B comforted her and told her it was okay to go. We kept her comfortable, surrounded by the love of family until later that day, when she slipped away from this world and into the eternal, loving arms of Jesus.

A couple of days later, people gathered for her celebration of life. A friend of mine who is a "seer"—meaning that she can see into the spirit realm—was there. She pulled me aside. She said that my Mom and Dad were both standing at the head of the casket. "They want to thank you for the send-off party. They look so happy together." What a gift.

At the funeral, I was blessed with yet another miracle.

I was able to keep it together while I gave the eulogy.

"Some of us call her 'Mom,' some 'Grandma' or 'Great Grandma.' Some call her 'Aunt' and others call her 'friend.' We all have one thing in common—we all love her.

"Mom has taught us all that family is not limited to those connected by blood... you didn't have to pass through her body to call her 'Mom,' and friendship is something that can last a lifetime. No matter your differences of opinions with friends or family, we need to support those we love. Some people have been her friend for more than half a century. What a wonderful blessing!

"This wonderful woman has taught me about faith... to have faith in God—He will never leave you or let you down—even if it feels that way.

There is always a divine plan for each of us. Have faith in yourself and faith in each other.

"Along with faith goes trust. Trust that no matter what, even as we go through the pain of loss that we feel and through the tears we shed, we will be okay.

"One thing we've all learned through the last few years of her life is the true meaning of the word, 'courage.' She fought the bravest fight with more grace than anyone I know as she struggled to beat this disease. She faced it with a positive attitude and a personal commitment to living her remaining days as fully as possible. She is truly the most courageous woman I know.

"During the last few days, as we have spent time with family and friends, there has been such an outpouring of love and compassion. It's so wonderful to see how many lives my mother has touched.

"One of the most touching things I've heard came from my great-nephew, my niece's firstborn. He said, 'Grandma is now with Poppie—telling him about me, my sister, and my baby brother. We never got a chance to meet him, so she's telling him all about us.'"

That's where I lost it for a moment. But gathered my composure and continued.

"Mom may not be here in body anymore, but she will always be in our hearts. This is not really 'goodbye,' it's more like, 'til we meet again.'

"Just like Aunt Rose would never say, 'goodbye.' Instead, she would say, 'I love you, and God Bless You.'

"I love you, Mom; God Bless You."

Years later, I've realized that the most poignant, most miraculous moment of the last few days of my mother's life that will stay with me forever happened two nights before she journeyed to heaven. It was when she told me my deceased relatives were "cooking the pasta for the party." From the look on her face, I could tell Mom saw them as if they were alive and well in her room.

Through her eyes, I was gifted a little glimpse of heaven.

Major to Master
by Rev. Sandra Kitt

There is always hope, no matter how bad the circumstances.

Waking up in the hospital ward, with tubes coming out of me everywhere I thought, "*What the hell happened?*"

I remembered I had some flu-like symptoms, and I vaguely remembered being loaded into the ambulance. That memory was the last conscious thought I'd had for more than two weeks, because of a drug interaction with prescription medicine I was taking.

Aspiration pneumonia meant I could not move, swallow, or talk.

I remember only a few things during this time; friends visiting during my breathing treatments for pneumonia and the smell of the nurse's breath after lunch. What changed everything for me was a visit from my minister, Rev. Dr. Temple Hayes. She looked me right in the eyes and said: "Blink your eyes if you are ready to get out of here and go home."

I blinked like there was no tomorrow; she squeezed my hand, and I knew I would be okay. Her vision and faith gave me hope for the very first time when it was so desperately needed.

After spending the first thirty days in the VA Nursing Home isolated with a C. diff infection, my actual work began. It was more than six weeks before I could sit up in a chair without passing out from the pain. Rehabilitation started with occupational, physical, and speech therapy every day. Progress was plodding; learning to sit up, talk, and get my hands and fingers to move was taxing. I remember the exhilaration of standing between the physical therapy bars for a whole nineteen seconds.

It was extremely difficult to keep on any weight because I could not swallow solid food, and all my liquids were thickened. My weight became so low, I eventually had to have a peg tube installed to feed me.

I loved being in the VA with my fellow veterans.

We made a group called "the Rat Pack" that all sat and ate together. Everyone was welcome, and veterans came and went. We watched out for one another and encouraged each other along the way. However, it was several months before I could eat solid food and join them. This camaraderie, along with visits from family and friends, helped make life bearable, despite the circumstances.

A volunteer came and played the piano every day at lunchtime. Every night before bed, I would turn the radio on and sing to the oldies. Even though I could not talk, singing was easier and more fun. There were always activities available to take part in, and we went on field trips for dinners to different Disabled American Veterans posts. Being taken on a bike ride, playing soccer, and balloon volleyball were just a few of my fun activities. A favorite field trip was to the circus; I was so happy to be alive and acted like a little kid.

Going home in a wheelchair after five months in the VA was a bittersweet experience.

It was like rolling into a home that looked familiar but felt unfamiliar. Many changes had happened in everyone's life during this time while I was stuck in survival mode. Others had moved on with their lives. At the hospital, there had been patients or staff around twenty-four hours a day. Upon returning home, the isolation was unbearable, especially since it was difficult to get out of the house or even talk on the phone.

Food was still an issue in so many ways. Going to the grocery store was overwhelming, and nothing tasted the same. Since I never knew what would taste good, I ate the same things over and over. I ate coconut shrimp and spinach pizza for six months, just because I knew I would like it.

Once home, I decided the more I could do for myself, the quicker I would recover—a great idea in theory, but I needed so much help, it was not very practical. With little strength, the slightest movement was risky without help. Falling might be deadly and undo all my progress. I slept in a recliner for my first few months at home and usually watched television until three a.m. Several "face-plants" happened during this time, like planting my face on a coffee table or the floor because I lacked the core strength to transfer from the wheelchair to the chair. This would become a common occurrence over the next several years.

The first day I stayed home alone, I thought I smelled smoke and called someone to come over, even though I knew it was probably just in my head. It was just in my head. A fire was the one thing I feared the most, knowing I lacked the strength to open a window or the coordination and speed to get outside quickly.

When I first came home, I had had a helper twenty-four hours a day. Now the helpers only stayed for twelve hours, four days a week. They left water and snacks in the refrigerator's door so that I could reach them.

To learn to walk with a walker, I needed to be in physical therapy. But because I was so uncoordinated and had poor balance, I had to wait. They suggested walking back and forth in the swimming pool for coordination improvement. I did it daily.

I was surprised to realize I could stand without holding onto anything when a friend came over and helped me do yoga. Growing tired of waiting for physical therapy, I went to Goodwill and bought a walker, because I had things to do.

The mental challenges were just as bad as the physical ones.

Unsure of my memory or ability to think clearly, I started using the Lumosity Brain Training app to improve and measure my brain capabilities. All the measurements for the initial assessment were under twenty percent for my age group. The worst ones were speed, flexibility, and memory in that order. These challenges affected everything I did and simple tasks took inordinate amounts of time, making me late for everything.

Frustration became my best friend. I overreacted to everyday situations because I could not do the things once done with ease. I resisted accepting my situation as it was because I was constantly getting better. Most of the time, others could see my progress before I could, and I had to learn to celebrate the smallest improvements. Walking with a rolling walker was exciting and freeing. My newfound freedom made me hungry for more.

My driver's license had never been taken away, so one brave helper offered to give me driving lessons. Learning to drive all over again was like being a teenager. Developing confidence and learning to brake smoothly were the most challenging parts of the process. We spent six months practicing on the back roads around my neighborhood. Finally, venturing out in the car on my own posed new challenges, including getting the walker into the vehicle.

The first couple of times, I carefully crawled into the back seat, pulled the walker behind me, and then tried to crawl into the driver's seat. I finally figured out how to do it by pushing the fourteen-pound walker into the back seat and then hung onto the car's roof-rack to get into the driver's seat. I was free!

This new freedom allowed me to attend classes and events.

Church was my haven, a place to be with friends who were positive, encouraging, and gave me hope. When I felt ready to give up, someone always had an encouraging word. Coming back home to be alone was a letdown. A secret I kept was I had panic attacks every time I walked into the house at evening's end, because I knew it would be the last time I would see anyone that day. I wasn't comfortable being by myself.

Growing up, I had loved playing sports, and now I used this motivation as therapy. There is so much adaptive equipment available. I found that everyone can take part in just about any sport, including hand cycling, kayaking, and sailing. After gaining strength, I started horseback riding, water skiing, and snow skiing. Each success gave me the courage to try the next, more challenging sport, like downhill skiing.

A poster at the Veterans Hospital advertising a winter sports clinic, led to my first time skiing. It was the most motivational experience of my life. There are no words to describe the view at 13,000 feet, knowing you are getting ready to ski downhill—possibly very fast. It was and still is so inspirational and humbling to see quadriplegics and blind veterans ski. We also got to take part in sled hockey, snowmobiling, and many other winter activities. But snow skiing remains my favorite sport. I try to go at least once a year.

Five years before my incident, I had been a chaplain. Afterwards, because of my limitations, I couldn't fulfill those duties. My healing allowed me to resume my chaplain role. It was a fantastic way to give of myself, and while praying with and for others, I was also healing myself. I also got certified in Reiki healing during this time and learned so much about energy medicine. The chaplain retreats were a powerful and safe place to connect, heal, and grow.

My focus on others distracted me from my challenges and allowed me to realize I was not as bad off as I had thought. Since I love learning, I wanted to return to college, mainly to see if I could do it. I enrolled in St. Petersburg College, where I had attended thirty years earlier. Classes there now required massive computer work. Although it took me extra time and work with a tutor, I kept up with the course work and became certified in graphic art.

I realized that if I put my mind to it, I could do anything.

Music had been a big part of my life and an essential part of my healing process. I'd learned to read music in high school while playing multiple instruments. Taking piano and drum lessons for several years after my accident helped my eye-hand coordination and dexterity. It was so enjoyable I bought a keyboard and still practice at home. Being able to create music again is such great therapy for me.

As an avid bike rider, I had competed in riding competitions and even a one-hundred-mile long-distance ride. After my accident, I needed aerobic exercise. Biking was a fun way for me to get my heart rate up. A regular bike was still too difficult, but a reclining, recumbent bike worked. I still ride weekly. Even though I cannot walk quickly or run at all, when I'm on my bike, I can really go.

During my healing journey, I tried traditional therapy, energy healing, and even therapies developed specifically for brain injuries. The conventional therapies were helpful, but they only went so far. Some of my energy healing included theta healing, Reiki, and raindrop therapy, a combination of Native American and Reiki healing.

Strength training, aerobic exercise, and yoga were among the physical therapies I tried, and I still go to the gym five days a week. Several brain injury therapies were helpful, like the hyperbaric oxygen chamber, interactive metronome, and methylated vitamin B shots.

Some of my friends invited me to join a brain injury support group at my local hospital. It was the first time I was around people with my same issues, and I was able to see people worse off than I was. What surprised me most was learning how people had experienced brain injuries and hearing stories much more severe than my own. I also heard the caregiver's perspective of their job concerning the patient's all-consuming desire for a "normal life" again. For several years, I went to a Brain Injury Clubhouse, where we used arts and crafts to heal ourselves and connect with others.

During Covid-19, I worked on my licensed minister's certificate with the Institute for Leadership and Lifelong Learning International. This journey allowed me even more healing and transformation than I thought possible. I went within myself at a much deeper level and learned to be a heart-centered leader and difference-maker. They allowed me to speak in front of a worldwide audience and share my story of healing, which fulfilled my lifelong dream of becoming a Reverend.

When I reflect on my life, I see how many moments in time brought me to this point. Dealing with emotional turmoil most of my life set me up for the mayhem. In contrast, my professional life as a major in the Army, computer engineer, and teacher had provided invaluable skills for my long recovery road. They taught me discipline, patience, and determination, yet gave me the vision to see endless possibilities. But my most significant growth and healings have been my inner spiritual work in recovery programs and metaphysics.

Over the past ten years, I have healed in so many ways.

Even though I still use a walker, I have come a long way. Mental and emotional healing has been just as important as physical healing to me. I have learned that my attitude will carry me through the worst of times by allowing me to see the light at the end of the tunnel when my journey is at its darkest. It has taken a village to support me in this process, and I am grateful for everyone who helped me along the way.

My biggest learned lesson is this: "There is always hope, no matter how bad the circumstances." Another lesson was that no matter how bad off I may be, there is always someone who has it far worse. We cannot always see people's challenges, so I've learned to be kind to everyone and grateful for everything. When I am grateful for what I have, even the small victories, then I can move through the challenges to the healing, become the master of my own life, and follow my dreams to live my miracle.

Having Faith
by Jill Landry

I saw with greater clarity a bigger purpose at play.

My name is Faith, and I am a twelve-year-old German Shepherd. For most of my life, I lived with my person in a small home. She loved and took care of me, and I loved her very much and took my job of watching over her seriously. She was my world, and I was hers. We were happy.

When I was seven years old, my world expanded, and a new family member came into my life—my dog sister, Summer. I took care of her, too. I loved that I had a friend to play with and now had someone else to watch over. My person was getting older, and she couldn't run around with me as much. Summer and I had so much fun playing together. We were always together with our person, day and night.

In September 2016, my world quickly changed.

My person was there with us; and then she wasn't. I knew she hadn't been feeling well. I was closely connected to her and I sensed something was off. But I didn't know she would be gone so soon. It happened so

fast. People came into the house that I didn't know, and Summer and I were scared. They took us to a strange place with lots of barking dogs.

Summer and I were separated. I could still see her at times, but we weren't together in the way we were before. The people thought that would be best. I am a smart and intuitive dog, but I didn't understand this. I became a good observer, watching people walk back and forth all day from the small area where my bed was. I kept wondering what was happening. The people taking care of me were kind, but they weren't my person. This was a big change for me! My world had been so small before—my home, my person, and Summer. Now everything was different.

Sometimes people would come and spend time with me and take me for walks. They would talk about adopting me. I listen closely! There's a lot you can learn by listening to other people's conversations. I understood a lot of words, but I didn't really know what "adoption" meant. Then it happened.

One day, I met my "now" people: my new family.

I wasn't so sure about them at first. I was hesitant and took my time to observe them before getting close. I sensed that this might be a good fit, but I wanted to check them out more before making any commitments. They came several times to visit with me and they were very respectful of my space. They let me come to them. When I did, they gave me lots of treats and love. I started to think this might work out okay. Everybody in this place was kind and they did such a great job of taking care of me, but I missed being in a real home and having someone to watch over. I decided to adopt this new family and loved having two new people to watch over.

I've been with my "now" people for a little more than two years. One of my new moms told me that when she first saw my picture online, she knew immediately she had to meet me. She told me of the very special dog that had been in their lives several years before me. I could feel their pain of losing Barstow; just like I hurt for the loss of my person and Summer. She knew I was special, and she was willing to open her heart again to loving another dog. And I knew that these were two very special people, for me to be willing to open my heart again to love and trust them.

I still miss my first person very much, but I know she is still with me and is watching over me, making sure that I am taken care of. My new people got in touch with Summer's new people, and I got to see her again! I now know that she is loved, safe, happy, and taken care of. I no longer need to worry about her; and it all feels like it's the way it's supposed to be.

Even though I went through a change I wouldn't wish for anyone, I'm grateful to have found my new people who love me so much. I never thought I could love anyone as much as I loved my first person and Summer. I never thought my heart would heal after such great loss. But I'm finding that my heart is a lot bigger than I ever knew. There is room in it to love all of them.

There continued to be a lot of change in my life as I've experienced changes in my body.

My limbs have been getting weaker and I've learned to use a wheeled cart to help me walk. It has surely been a journey of courage, faith, and love. I've always wondered why my first person named me Faith. Maybe she knew that I was destined for something very special.

I've been teaching my new people so much about having faith. And that's not just about living with me, although there is a lot to say about that! Even though I need help to get outside, I have my part in the process too. A new trick I have recently learned is to open doors with my nose. And you know what is interesting about that—in life, too—is that Faith Opens Doors.

Many beautiful things can happen, even in the midst of change and difficult circumstances. Besides doors, I know I am here on this Earth to open hearts. I have certainly opened the hearts of my people, and they have opened mine. I hope that through sharing my story, many more hearts will be opened. It's amazing how the threads of deep pain, sorrow, and loss, when woven into a bigger tapestry, can create such a beautiful picture, all guided by something greater. The opportunity to see the beauty is always there, but you might miss it if you aren't looking with your heart and the eyes of faith. Together, we are re-writing what was a tragedy into a beautiful story of healing and love.

Faith made her transition into spirit at 12 ½ years old.

She experienced complications from both degenerative myelopathy and cancer. Due to the degenerative myelopathy, her body progressively weakened over a two-year period, until she reached the point where she needed support and assistance for all daily activities for the last six months of her life. Despite the weakness in her body, her spirit was strong, and she continued to be engaged in life.

I became her constant side-by-side companion, and my daily routine revolved around caring for her. While I am so grateful that I had the ability, knowledge, and time to support Faith on her journey in this way, it was extremely challenging physically, mentally, and emotionally. There

132

was so much uncertainty from day to day, and there were moments I questioned all of it. But as much as I was taking care of her, it wasn't until after she had passed that I realized just how much she had been taking care of me too.

The loss of Faith's physical presence left a gaping hole in my heart and in my life. Faith had become my joy, purpose, and meaning; my reason for getting up each morning. With her passing, I felt lost.

I began a deep journey with grief.

As I dived deeper into grief, I experienced profound sadness, anger, regret, resentment, denial, and fear in varying intensities at different times. There were ups and downs, and I learned to ride the waves as best as I could when they came.

During this time, I found myself in my own crisis of faith, accompanied by shame for struggling so much. I came to realize that I might have been carrying unresolved grief with me for a very long time. My grief deepened with additional losses of a significant relationship, a friend with cancer, and a home. I had come to know and define myself, but my life was unraveling at an alarming rate.

I had always spoken about how having Faith in my life spoke so deeply to me about having *faith* on a bigger life scale. But now I was questioning everything about my life and whether I was going to choose to have faith to continue with it. Life had become full of pain, grief, and loss. I was processing it all, and then processing it again.

Was there something to live for beyond what seemed like a never-ending process of dealing with grief? I was struggling to see beyond the cycle I felt caught in.

Despite some very low moments, I kept moving forward, step by step, with many helpers, as I asked for understanding, purpose, and meaning. Then I heard an interview with Michael Bernard Beckwith that significantly shifted my process of grieving in a matter of fifteen minutes. He said, "When we are in the lowest ebb of grief, we usually ask, what is the meaning of this? Why did this happen? But we can reverse the question and instead ask, based on this person being in my life, how can I give my life meaning?"

While the emotions associated with loss are valid and real, when I asked the second question, my experience began to transform and I recognized that this could become something so much bigger than just my own loss.

With this perspective, I could see that the pain and grief we experience with loss can have a purpose. It can be a transformative process, bringing deeper meaning, purpose, and richness into my life—if I choose to allow it. I can embrace new meaning in my life because Faith was in it; because I loved her deeply and even because of, not in spite of, the loss I have experienced. What that is, and the form it takes, is up to me.

Mine is Faith.

Faith, my dog, taught me about faith, forgiveness, and unconditional love. Through our soul-level connection, she reflected back to me a light I had not seen in myself. One of her greatest messages to me was about having faith in myself—a message that came to me through the first picture I saw of her, two months before we met. She gifted me faith in more ways than one.

As I've walked the path with grief, I have discovered how to start walking toward a path of joy, which has led me to a new city. The first night I arrived, I had a glimpse of how the universe was conspiring, before I had any conscious recognition of it, to bring me to this point so I could further my journey of self-discovery.

In that moment, instead of only seeing the grief, loss, and all the challenges I had been through, I connected with the magic of how all of that had been woven together in a way that I could have never scripted on my own. Faith's transition and the timing of it, as well as other losses and events that have unfolded since then, all played into the process of opening the doors for me to be here now.

As I saw with greater clarity a bigger purpose at play, I began to find gratitude for all of it, in a way that I would have never thought was possible a year before. The experiences I went through in loving Faith and losing her physical presence, and the other experiences of loss that followed, unearthed the recognition of something deeper within me: a part of me that did feel enough, that was courageous, that was ready, and that could step into something new with faith.

The joy, meaning, and purpose that Faith brought to my life is not gone just because she is no longer physically with me. It is just taking on another form. She is still teaching me, and I'm beginning to find my faith again.

Tragedy to Triumph
by Karuna

I received fierce Grace.

All was going so well, I was pinching myself as I drove up the road to my beautiful mountain home in the high country above Boulder, Colorado. My son had been visiting me from London with his newlywed before they moved to San Francisco. We had precious time to enjoy each other, sit by the fire, and drink in the view of the mountain peaks that form the horizon along my back deck.

Alone again, I was weaving back up my mountain road, crossing the pavement and then the gravel, returning to my pastoral home of more than thirty years. The sunny days while my son and new daughter-in-law had been with me were now turning to rain. It seemed almost fitting as an end to what had been such a wonderful time.

As I came around my greenhouse and shed, to pull into the driveway where I would normally be greeted by the bright blue window boxes that frame the windows of my house, something both strange and incomprehensible came into sight. Oddly enough, it was Halloween and, like something from a Halloween movie, all the windows of my house were frosted over *from within*. I immediately knew something extremely odd, or even terrible, must have happened.

It was the strangest thing I had ever seen.

I immediately ran to the front door, which would usually open into my large, windowed, greeting room. I was on alert—but not prepared for what I would see. Torrents of water were running and spraying down from all the levels of my house as if in a violent, interior rainstorm. I stood there in shock. Was this happening? I had never seen anything like this in my life.

Then it hit me that I had better move fast and figure out what to do first. That moment was like a sudden slideshow flashing through both my mind and mind's eye. I recalled lessons I had learned from my years of devoted yoga practice: *stability, alertness,* and *calm.* Instead of paying attention to my immediate human emotions, which were telling me to yell, shout, cry out, or just run around, I was able to become very calm and simply ask myself "Okay, how do I react usefully?"

The phone was working, so I called a neighbor who I thought might know what was behind all this. They told me to immediately shut off my well, since it was likely something had gone horribly wrong with the water system. I did that and then immediately called my insurance company. I figured they would have a "bead" on what was going on and could advise me what to do next.

It was then that it hit me.

I took a deep breath and absorbed the situation. Standing still, I looked around at everything with a bit of wonderment. The inevitable question then came across my mind: "Why did this happen?"

I suppose this is the question that nearly everyone would ask in this kind of sudden, seemingly inexplicable, disaster. So, it was *my turn*. These thoughts bubbled around in me for the hour it took for the insurance personnel to arrive. Immediately, relief came with the assurance they gave me. I had done nothing wrong; it was not my fault, and my insurance would cover all of what appeared to be quite a major disaster.

I still could not quit asking myself *why* this had happened—especially on the heels of such a wonderful set of days with my family, in my lovely home—a house which, in nearly thirty years, had not endured any major disruption or damage at all. Had I made some mistake? Was this because I hadn't done "this" or "that"? Was this "payback" for God-knows-what? Was the *feng shui* off? Had my house been crying out for help, and I had not listened?

I received fierce Grace.

From the fierce, yet amazingly bountiful, Grace of this experience, I received my "doctor's degree" in rejecting the tendency to play the "analysis game," the "why game," or the "blame game."

I have been lucky to live the last decades of my life within a spiritual community. I work with wonderful people in the context of beautiful worldviews, and lifestyles based on love, mutuality, reciprocity, kindness, compassion, and on and on. I think, over the years, I got used to thinking that it was these contexts that made these people and the way they lived so special. After all, I was also a teacher. So, actually, I was spending my life "teaching others" about these ways of life—about love, mutuality, reciprocity, kindness, compassion, and so on.

Imagine how side-swiped and flabbergasted I felt when—thrown out of my element, thrown out of my home, thrown out of my teaching center, and just "thrown out into the world"—suddenly here, among all these "strangers" were wonderful people running to help me. They were not claiming, or even referencing, any kind of spiritual reason for their goodness or good deeds, or some spiritual practice they had been immersed in to make them so giving and so caring. Just an amazing rush of people, full of love, caring, compassion, and a desire to help— irrespective of background or belief.

I was reminded of something I had forgotten.

In this disaster in my life, from which people could have just walked away or done what was the "token" required by their job or profession, I was gifted with a steady flow of caring and help from countless people. They came into this predicament from every angle: from the details of insurance, arrangements for temporary and then long-term accommodation, the meeting of immediate personal disaster needs (as all of my belongings were either destroyed or removed and sequestered), and then the plans and planning for restoring and rebuilding my home.

I had come to expect this kind of behavior from people of "spiritual practice, ethics and ideals," but I was overwhelmed by these unbelievable people—on this planet with me—who have never even heard of yoga, or this or that spirituality or religion. These people knew nothing about me or my past.

As I sat through the next months, helped by so many old and new friends, I was still not sure if or when I might be returning to my house.

During this time, while I lived first in a hotel and then in a "temporary" house, I knew I was processing through something "big" for me. I was operating completely outside my old element, going to courses, and classes and associations I had never even heard of before simply "because they were what's around," and knowing, all the time, that I was in this learning process about these lessons: "You're healthy," "You can do this," and "You can trust this." The most important lesson was: "This is not something you would have designed for yourself, but it was apparently designed for *you.*"

It has occurred to me that for all the "rebirthing classes" that I offered out of the yoga studio that was part of my home for twenty-seven years, I seemed now to have been offered the biggest "rebirthing" of my own! In the journey since, I, the person who was always helping others, has gotten to learn what it means to accept help from others. In amazement, I have experienced how freely that help has been offered and given. I can honestly now stand in my rebuilt house and say to myself, "If there are any such things, *this* was a meant to be."

Triumph Through Miracles
by Eileen Bild

With knowledge comes great responsibility.

lthough I've had my share of trials and tribulations, just when I thought I was done and life could become a walk in the park—somehow, I was blindsided once again.

I had overcome and was well into my healing from a multitude of incidences that happened all at once. A divorce, my mom passing away from cancer, a move to a new state where I did not know anyone, a new relationship, and working my way through hitting rock bottom and climbing my way out of the well. At the stage of recovery where my emotions were stable, my spirit was feeling better, and physical training was strengthening my body, I had yet another debilitating experience.

This one almost grounded me for good.

I woke up one morning with my arm swollen, feeling on fire and itching. Not having a clue as to what had happened, thinking maybe I had cat scratch fever (we have a Maine Coon cat), I administered some homeopathic remedies. This seemed to help for a day or two, but then the symptoms resurfaced with a vengeance. It took three trips to the doctor to determine I had been bitten, while sleeping at home, by a brown recluse spider.

Despite knowing I have what it takes to push through obstacles and trauma, the thought of having to go through a long healing process again was frustrating and disappointing. It made me downright angry. In the beginning, the pain was unbearable. The bite had activated a dormant auto-immune marker and my body began turning on itself, attacking my nervous system. Among the physical symptoms were excruciating migraines that showed up out of nowhere. At times, the pressure in my head was (and still is) so great, giving up was more appealing than crawling through each episode.

My husband felt so helpless, but there was nothing he could do. He knew I was in pain and suffering. However, something within me—a strength beyond my mental capacities—kept me going. I knew when the body is waging a war within, the healing must start within.

I was on my own...

The medical community does not have a full understanding of the mind/body/spirit connection. They just know to look at numbers, symptoms, and what pills to prescribe. I did not want to have a bandage; I wanted to heal and get my life back.

I spent hours, days, months poring through information, researching all I could to understand how to undo what the spider had done. My diligence kept me seeking and finding alternative practitioners who looked at the body as a whole. I found a great functional medicine doctor who performed a battery of tests and used the results to develop a protocol for me to follow. We discovered ways to turn off the "fire" in my body and work, layer by layer, to systematically stabilize my system.

I also started working with a nutritionist whose practice is based on muscle testing, an amazing technique that enables the body to tell us what it needs and the level of healing that has occurred, as well as how much further we need to go in the treatment. She also set forth a protocol for healing.

One miracle after another came into my life.

As a practitioner of the healing arts, I intuitively pay attention to how I feel and what my body is telling me. For each layer that was healed, I would feel an unmistakable shift. For the first two years, I could not eat much. Anything acidic, with vinegar, meat, or spices was inflammatory and not digestible.

My hyper-sensitivity to heat and the sun really disappointed me, as I am an outdoor, nature type of person. We could not go out on our boat and I could not enjoy the ocean and beach. I was devastated to lose those things. Being able to get back to enjoying these activities was a motivator to kick this in the @$$!

Miracle number one was the first time I could feel the sun on my face and not have a reaction. The discomfort of swollen lips, an overactive immune system, and blistering is weakening, and it took every ounce of my being to be patient and wait for the episodes to finish. This breakthrough was euphoric and kept hope alive that someday this ordeal would be in the past.

I continued to work and did video productions, living as normally as I could, but behind the façade of things seeming normal, I was fighting what sometimes felt like a losing battle. But I am a strong believer in when there is a will, there is a way! Every day, I prayed for an answer or a sign that the nightmare was just a dream gone sideways and when I woke up, I'd find life was just playing a twisted joke. Often, a part of me would scream at the universe, "This is not fair! Haven't I've been through enough?"

Some people will say that we are only given that which we can handle.

Well, although that might be true, it sure is a damn hard pill to swallow when you are given the burden of a sickness that feels like a searing hot fire you can't put out. While grateful for the knowledge that I am strong, resilient, and capable of handling some of the most challenging health issues, I have declared that I am done.

Over the years, I have wondered if something in my thinking led to this traumatic event and started me on a journey that has been arduous yet rewarding. For each miracle, each step forward in healing and higher awareness of my capacity to overcome, I find it in my heart to come to peace with the situation.

Miracle number two was when I could start working out again and felt my muscle strength increase. Again, no adverse reaction, only the determination to get my life back to where I want it. I have always taken care of my body, and it feels empowering to do strength training, see the results, and experience the renewed energy. This pushes me to continue to override the programming that has been installed in my system that weakens me. Some days, the motivation is not as powerful as I would like, and I must find something deep within to pull it through.

Each small step forward builds upon the larger leap I have made.

Sometimes, I take for granted the simple things in life. When dealing with this enemy within, which I cannot see and have no immediate control over, any small sign of triumph is a cause for celebration.

Miracle number three happened during dinner one night. I'd been avoiding red onions and had no desire to try them, but this evening, something changed. As I was putting salad on my plate, I had a strong urge to include the red onions. Hesitating, I went back and forth with that little voice inside arguing that it would not be good. But I ultimately surrendered. As soon as I bit into a small piece, I could feel this rush throughout my body, a sense of "yes," as if my body was thanking me and showing me at the same time that I had healed and peeled away yet another layer. It was so profound a feeling, I could not avoid sitting with this for a little bit and recognizing it as success. It was just a bite of an onion, but a huge stride forward in my healing.

Whenever I feel tired of fighting, even though it is not as severe as in the beginning, I remind myself that it is the journey. Someday, I will conquer the beast. I will be free to roam this earth outside the shadow of its grip. Instead of the battle within, I'll revel in the beauty of life itself. These miracles are nuggets of my truth, and I honor them as the north star guiding me back home in the dark of night. This truth is the authentic me, the very essence of my being clear and cleansed, raw and real.

Does all of this rattle my sense of self—my self-worth, self-confidence, and self-esteem? It can tug me down that rabbit hole from time to time. The more I sit quietly and just allow, the better the outcome I find. In the undoing of an unbending and relentless enemy within, I have become more aware of an illusionary aspect. Through the miracles, those moments of relief, I can sense there is something beyond the veil of this mystery.

I become more empowered each day I wake up, still alive and thriving. The dichotomy of the good and bad, the healthy and not healthy, the pain and the joy, and the success and the failures have a dance. When in the flow of the movements within this dance, I can relish in the positive and seek to not attach to the negative. For every episode of pain and discomfort, I encourage myself to remember who I am and why I am here, and to remember this is just another test of my strength and endurance.

Would I prefer a different journey? Sometimes, but then I would not be who I am and could not be the same source of light, hope, and inspiration for myself and others. With knowledge comes great responsibility. I learn every day as I grow older and transform the results of a simple spider bite. It is not easy, by any means. I know this, too, shall pass…

A True Awakening
by Barbara A. Bertucci

*A miracle is what happens when you wake up one day,
and you are there, and you don't recall all the
necessary steps it took to get you there.*

They say an awakening is either discovered organically or forced upon us. Mine was forced.

"Did I hear you correctly? I have breast cancer?" I said to myself as much as to the doctor. Imagine me, an athlete from an upper-middle-class family of doctors who thrived at every corner of life, being told, "You have breast cancer."

I could not believe my ears. I was in the Cancer Club. With three dire words, "You have cancer," I became a member of a club filled with sisters, to which and with whom I did not wish to belong. No way! Not me! Surely, they have me mixed up with someone else. Initially, I resisted this new reality. Yet as I kept hearing the outer echoes of "You have cancer," I realized my inner echo—"I want to live!"—was becoming greater and stronger, and screaming louder.

Life was comfortable.

That's what I told myself. I had found the American dream in my second marriage and was accumulating all the *things* we convinced ourselves are important for a happy and fulfilled life. But, as the years faded, I faded with them. Over time, I went from comfortable to uncomfortable to numb. It was like the story of the frog and the slow boil: Experts say a frog will jump out of hot water, but if you slowly heat the water, the frog will stay in there until its demise. The heating water will gradually take the frog over without it knowing it. That was me. I was the frog that had been taken over little by little... in the hot water.

My friends attempted to tell me, time and time again, that I was in a verbally abusive relationship.

Yet I would turn a deaf ear to them and the other cheek to my husband. We were too far down the marriage path to get out unscathed. As a means of escape, I was sleeping through the nightmare of constantly being yelled at and abused. But even as I tried to ignore it, the damage grew.

I had been heckled and bullied throughout my childhood by my brothers. Now I was living through screaming, condescension, and even violence in my adulthood. At that time, I was dying more than I was living, energetically speaking.

At the beginning of our marriage, we had moved to a town where we knew no one. There was no family support, and with him working long hours, it felt like I was a single parent, doing everything alone. I got a management job when I found myself expecting our first child, and then our second child. Wow! We were solidifying as a family for sure.

Cancer woke me up. Now I needed to figure out how to stay awake.

Growing up, we had moved during the beginning of my first grade… clear across town. Mom was thrilled that I had been accepted into a private Catholic school the year before. My questions to mom were, "Why am I being shipped off to a strange school? How come I can't go to the school where my brothers and sisters are going? What did I do wrong?"

Needless to say, I felt I was being punished. It left me with the core feeling that I was broken and had done something terribly wrong.

Feeling broken was a burden I carried all my life, until the day the cancer was removed.

The nun at my first grade forced me to write with my right hand although I was naturally left-handed. She would not listen as I shared my feelings, and her ruler on my hand spoke louder than any words. When I did get a chance to speak out at school, my classmates made fun of me because I talked differently due to my accent from the "other part of town."

My heckling remained hidden. As the baby of nine children, half of the time, my family didn't even know where I was, let alone create a space for me to share my daily feelings or school experience.

When my mom finally realized what the nun had done, I spent the whole summer with a patch on my right eye to switch me back to my correct, left-eye dominance. But although I practiced writing again with my left hand, it was too late. I couldn't switch back or undo what had been done to me. The mixed messages to my brain even affected my reading ability.

Although I had been tested by a psychologist and labeled a genius, the scars from my youth outweighed my ability to be a highly functional student. I was going to have to repeat fifth grade.

"Please let me attend my sister's boarding school," I begged my mom, so I wouldn't have to feel like a failure at this same school. Once away at this school, I was able with persistence to work ahead. Eventually, I skipped the seventh grade and returned to my regular grade level, yea!

I suffered greatly from sibling abuse.

My older brother had explored his sexuality with me. When I shared the secrets of all that had occurred, no one believed me. Maybe, on some level, they did believe me—yet they never responded. Then suddenly, one day, all the girls in the family got locks on their bedroom doors.

It was the beginning of my thinking: *Barbara is broken.* I would continue to attract people into my life for many years who reminded me of this inner belief. True healing happens when trust and validation are present. I had lived my entire life with neither.

After my cancer diagnosis, when I began to fight for my life, I started to look back and understand. As I looked around to envision what life could be on the other side of this disease, I was drawn to people in recovery who were living as spiritual seekers.

In my own way, I had always felt spiritual and connected to God, but I'd never really witnessed Spirit through my religious upbringing in the Catholic faith. Saying the rosary or a novena hadn't brought me closer to God. Talking with Him and my spirit guides, or the angels, and asking them for guidance and direction was my way of connecting with God.

My miracle manifested when I found a God who was perfect for me.

Through this reality, I began to be there for myself as well. I started to believe that I might not be broken after all, and I discovered the Unity way. I became a chaplain at First Unity Spiritual Campus in St. Petersburg. With a small group of people, during a retreat, I began to open doors to my soul and once again connect with God. I began to feel that I am worthy of love and being loved.

In the church, I started understanding and accepting that I was not a mistake, because I'd found a home where I could become whole, find myself, and accept myself as I am. But, most importantly, I found a home inside myself.

I felt comfortable again, and this time, my comfort was not based on external realities, but on an inner love and appreciation of myself. It was a true awakening.

Now, as a seventeen-year cancer-free thriver who has found true love and a supportive partner, I am becoming the role model for my children and grandchildren that I have always longed to be.

I love the saying: "A miracle is what happens when you wake up one day, and you are there, and you don't recall all the necessary steps it took to get you there." Cancer woke me up, and waking up brought me the miracle of my own life. My journey was a long one, from mayhem to a miracle, and I thank God every day for my blessings.

Final Thoughts

Despite fires, floods, spider bites, and even death, one miracle after another came into the author's lives. This section was full of grit, grace, faith, and hope. All the stories expressed gratitude for the small victories of overcoming mayhem. It was important to many authors, including pets, to become the master of their own life and destiny. The stories showed us that there was always a bigger purpose at play, and the players had to have faith and hope in a positive outcome, even if it was a glimpse of Heaven.

PART 4

LIFE JOURNEY AND IDENTITY
The Long and Winding Road

It is time to dance.
We have surrendered to our dance.
Your dance is waiting to begin.

The Hope to Go On
by Rev. Ariel Patricia

I did matter to someone.

Life was hard. Unfortunately, even with the best of intentions, it was becoming evident that my emotional health was going to get worse before it got better. I was handling day-to-day living, but most days, I was filled with sadness; some days, I was filled with despair, and on others, I was filled with both. I called myself a functioning depressive.

It wasn't that I wasn't trying.

My feelings of worthlessness clung to me. The pep talks everyone gave me weren't helping. I knew they meant well, but they didn't really understand. How could they? They didn't see the real me. I put on a brave face, and for the most part, it succeeded. Sometimes people saw the cracks, but only the cracks on the surface. They didn't realize that so many of those cracks led to deep crevices and dark chasms.

I didn't realize it either, until one particularly depressing day. It was the kind of afternoon that could leave anyone feeling down. The sun was setting in a cloudy, cheerless, late-winter sky. As the afternoon winds down, you feel confused as to how to spend your time. It's not nighttime, so you can't start to relax from the day's activities, but it's too dark to feel like it's afternoon, so you're left feeling out of sorts. I didn't know what to do, so I just sat at my kitchen table, feeling especially sad.

I had recently decided that it really didn't matter if I was around or not. I could leave that day, and sure, some people would miss me, or maybe even be sad for a time—but they would be fine. I listed everyone that I was close to, from my kids to my mom, my siblings, and my friends. I convinced myself that I wasn't the most important person to any of them, or to anyone, actually. So, what was the point?

Then, as God would have it, my daughter Megan came downstairs and sat down.

"What's wrong, Mom?" she asked.

I knew I shouldn't be dumping all of my emotional stuff on my fourteen-year-old. I'm ashamed to say, I did anyway.

"I could leave tomorrow and no one would really notice," I replied.

"What?" Megan asked, sounding very confused.

"I could leave tomorrow, and sure, some people would be sad, but everyone would be fine," I explained. "I'm not the most important person to anyone." I had finally voiced aloud what had been in my heart for a long time.

"Mom, what are you talking about?" Megan asked hurriedly.

She quickly started naming everyone I was close to. For everyone she listed, I had an answer. I had already figured this out. "No, she has so-and-so. No, he has so-and-so," I kept responding.

"Well, what about me and Lindsey?" Megan asked, sounding a little scared.

"You and Lindsey have your aunt and grandmother. You will be fine," I assured her.

"But they're not my mom!" she cried, very upset now. "Mom, even if the only person that you matter to is ME, aren't I enough?" Tears spilled down her cheeks.

"You're my mom!" she went on. "Aren't I enough?"

In that instant, I heard my own words coming from my daughter's mouth.

"Oh, my goodness! Megs, don't cry!" I said feeling a little panicked. "Of course, you're enough! You're more than enough!"

For the first time in a long time, I began to feel something through my fog of sadness. Megan made me realize that someone really did care about me. I did matter to someone. Slowly, I started to care again, too.

I had to; Megan was depending on me.

If Megan had never sat down at the kitchen table that day, I don't know where I would be. She gave me the hope to go on. It's been a long and winding road, but ten years later, I am a different person—living a life filled with purpose and a passion for the future.

We Are All Chosen

by James Redfield

*When we practice giving consciously, our lives begin
to move forward faster. Everything amplifies.*

Sometimes, even now, I'm amazed *The Celestine Prophecy* ever happened. I still remember dozens, maybe even hundreds, of unlikely events that had to occur to bring the Story to the world. You see, my life before the book was beyond chaotic, as I struggled to cope with being kicked out of college…. Well, I wasn't actually *kicked out* of college. It was just that no one wanted to loan me any more money to jump from one esoteric interest to another, trying to find my place in life.

Yet, for those of you who are out there searching, there is hope.

I did finally find my niche, but again, in ways, that now seem unbelievable. So much so, in fact, that for a long time after the book was published, I didn't talk much about how it happened.

Most people don't remember the stir "The Book" caused when it first came out. Who would have believed that such a deeply esoteric first novel would hang around on The New York Times Best Sellers List for three years? Moreover, it was the number one American book in the world for two of those years.

And everyone wanted to know how I did it.

I was embarrassed, I guess, because telling my experience of how the book happened made it seem as though I'd been chosen in some way, and I didn't like the way that sounded. It wasn't the message I wanted to send, or the message of the book.

The message of *The Celestine Prophecy* is that we can *all* find a flow of synchronistic help in this world that works, that uplifts what we expect from life and shows us our dream work in the world.

When we find that flow, it feels like nothing short of Destiny... something meant to be... what we had come here to do all along.

At the time, I didn't want to comment about all that. The truth was, *The Celestine Prophecy*—and later, the other books—were delivering that truth quite well on their own, without me being the focus.

Now, however, the situation is different. The book has been passed around for a long time, and it still is. You might even say it's had a resurgence because of what is happening in the world now.

More importantly, I don't worry about these kinds of appearances anymore. What happened, happened.

So, if you want to know more about how *The Celestine Prophecy* came to be... really... here it is. I'll tell you everything I possibly can.

As I mentioned, the book rose out of the ashes of my attempts at finding my chosen work. Not only did I get thrown out of college, but I had been thrown out of church, too. I had asked so many questions as a teenager that all the Sunday School teachers ran away from me.

Don't get me wrong. I grew up in one of the most supportive and authentic churches I've seen. I just wanted more information than they had.

I was asking questions such as: "If Adam and Eve were the first people on Earth, to whom did their sons get married?" Or "Why are there plainly described UFOs in the Book of Ezekiel in the Bible?" Or "What is the *real* definition of Spirituality?"

In response, they gave me a college kickoff party a year early. I kid you not.

And who could blame them?

When I first stepped into the university, I thought I had found my playground. Yet, I ultimately discovered that college teachers were just as reluctant to explore the higher questions about life and existence as people in general.

And then I began to read about a new, informal system of inquiry being recognized on the west coast called the *Human Potential Movement*, a semi-organized stream of research into the higher questions of human existence that began where orthodox science had left off… or rather, had quit.

I couldn't have been more excited! But to continue this story, we need to delve for a moment into the history of Science itself.

No one teaches this anymore, but Academic Science gained traction when Western Religion was exposed to be unbelievably corrupt.

Science was launched to study how the natural world actually worked.

And in the beginning, there was great hope that science would study everything, not merely the physical world, but the larger Cosmology of the Universe—and, of course, the Psychological and Religious/Spiritual nature of Humanity.

Science started where it found itself, looking out on an unexplored material world and wondering how it all operated. And they stayed with that focus, mapping out every aspect of the physical world around us... until they had so thoroughly described the world as secular, explained, and predictable that they themselves couldn't imagine there being anything else going on. So eventually, they declared that science was mostly finished... at least as far as the public was concerned.

As time passed, the public started to believe this as well, and naturally began to concentrate on utilizing this material world to gain wealth and material security. As never before, they could sleep soundly at night because all the crazy superstitions about physical reality had been resolved.

When it came time to explore the rest of the human experience, they naively said they couldn't find any evidence of Spiritual Consciousness in humans—or any consciousness at all, for that matter. All perception was reduced to the random firings of the brain.

Even Psychology reduced the higher questions to studying the behavior of people, and Religion itself began to focus not on the Transcendent Experience, but on the material goals of social improvement.

In the end, Science began to proclaim outright that the world is meaningless and without purpose. Scientists completely quit their search for the higher answers about life.

To my disbelief, that was all I found in college, at first. Academic disciplines were focusing only on the outer world.

For a long time, the true progress of Science had been... well, stymied.

Until, that is, the arrival of one Carl Gustav Jung.

Without Jung, there would not have been the "opening up" of the budding science of psychology. No Human Potential Movement, and certainly no *Celestine Prophecy* book.

You see, Jung risked everything to break away from Freud's lame, materialistic theories that reduced the whole of human experience to an "Oedipus Complex," where we were held back and doomed forever because we had to repress our unconscious sexual desire for our opposite-sex parent!

Jung, on the other hand, demanded we explore the complete range of human consciousness, including Spiritual Connections, our Intuitive faculties... and to my budding appreciation, the Phenomenon of "Synchronicity."

When Jung made that stand, I found out, he *de facto* began the long Human Potential Movement, which was solely dedicated to exploring the highest reaches of our potential consciousness.

I couldn't wait to dive into the history of this movement. Jung considered Synchronicity as nothing short of a real "Operating Principal" in human life. He defined it as the "Experience of Meaningful Coincidences," and as you know, *The Celestine Prophecy* champions the experience of Synchronicity.

Jung infused the Movement with a legitimacy that inspired a century-long trail of thinkers, poets, scholars, mystics, and yes, rigorous scientists, all of whom wondered why Academic Science had stopped exploring the esoteric world. They wanted to find new answers about how the many facets of Spiritual Consciousness really worked. That's what I wanted, too.

I should add that it was Jung's discovery of Synchronicity that finally began to break the "spell of Secular Materialism" in the world, which will eventually be known as the most iron-clad example of "Group Think" in human history.

The Phenomenon of Synchronicity, once seen for oneself as valid, had the effect of awakening humanity to a new, more inspired life.

Why? Because, if Synchronicity—those mysterious coincidences that open little doors of opportunity toward a destined life—really exists, it means we live in a world where we get metaphysical "help" in life.

And that could only happen if we live in a Spiritual World, not a material one.

But I'm getting a bit ahead of the story. At this point, even as I digested all the information I could find in the history of the HPM, I was still asking, "What's *my* life work?"

As I mentioned, I had lingered in a graduate level, Department of Education, Community Counseling curriculum for as long as I could afford, when a Synchronicity suddenly led me into a job helping challenged adolescents who had wound up on the wrong side of the law. Our program was their last stop before a trek to prison, and we initiated Spiritually-based interventions that worked.

By then, I knew this position was destined in my preparation—but I also knew there was something else I was supposed to do. Suddenly, I felt stuck, so I whimsically decided to embark on a Vision Quest (no lie) deep into the woods, in the Cherokee tradition, which my mother told me I had the genes for.

When I had walked two miles into a national forest, I set up camp and sat back against a tree to appreciate the quietness of nature and one of the most gorgeous sunsets I can remember.

And that's when I had the *Vision*. (See? I told you.)

Believe me, if I could call this experience anything but a vision, I would. It was akin to a daydream, maybe, but longer and more gripping, as classic visions usually are.

Here's what I saw: It was me, years ahead in time. I was experiencing a huge "moment of Inspiration" to write a book. The vision included a memory about my background experiences with writing. I had won back-to-back, county-wide essay contests in middle school and several awards in high school.

Those had really occurred, but I had dismissed them to the extent they were completely lost to my memory. In the Vision, I understood why. To my family, setting out to be an author was like signing up to be an astronaut. It just wasn't included in the realm of possibility.

But in the Vision, my Inspiration had paid off, and in a series of detailed scenes, I saw myself starting from scratch and being helped out by one Synchronicity after another. I discovered the material that should be in the book, and the style of the writing, and how I would discover the best way to publish, and then how to publicize the work.

Further, I saw what could occur if I kept the faith. I watched the book climb the bestseller lists locally, nationally, and then internationally.

With that, the Vision ended.

I was still sitting with my back against the same tree. The birds were chirping around me. The sunset seemed to be at about the same stage, still lighting up the western sky. I was back!

What did I think?

I shook my head and thought I'd had the biggest pipe dream in the world. I even went home a day early, hearing my high school principal in my head, saying, "Do something practical with your life."

For months, that was my attitude. *Who are you to write a book, anyway?* I thought. After all, I had no clue what it would be about. My counseling practice was doing okay. So I told myself to forget about that daydream.

Then, one day, a client, out of the blue, told me I should write a book. I suddenly felt a level of Inspiration Energy that brought back the memory of the Vision.

For the first time, I started to take writing more seriously.

I spent some time traveling to clear my head. And that's when I ran into a string of rumors about various old documents that spelled out an awakening of Humanity through a series of Transcendent Experiences the public would discover. There was no way to source these prophecies, but they seemed to mirror much of the findings being made in the Human Potential Movement.

Questions filled my head. Was all this Synchronistic to my journey? Was a consensus about Spiritual Consciousness already forming from the HPM research in its hundred years of exploration? Was the guy kicked out of college and church, the one to write about it?

With that thought, another memory busted though, sending my Inspiration soaring. Wow, I remember thinking it with a shiver. I was now figuring out what the book was going to be about. Something I saw in the Vision.

It was all beginning to come true in real life, right before my eyes.

I dove in with an even deeper study of the HPM and found a consistent trail through all the significant Spiritual Experiences that seemed to be available to each of us, and they seemed to occur in understandable steps.

As you read forward, you might recognize them in their final form as the core Insights of the Book, but at this point, I was merely pulling them together.

Jung had discovered Synchronicity, the hand of fate and destiny, which brings us mysterious help in life. And the HPM seemed to be pointing to these other Experiences as have the role of *increasing our Synchronicity*. The more of these Experiences that we integrated into our lives, the faster our Synchronicity toward our personal missions could flow.

The messages of so many of these explorers were similar: Any of us now could prove to ourselves that these Experiences are real, just by intending to find them in our lives.

Then I discovered one of the most important of these additional Experiences: moving into alignment with the apparent Karmic Design of our world. It all seemed to revolve around the power of helping, or giving, to others.

When we practice giving consciously, our lives begin to move forward faster. Everything amplifies.

When we help others, we can find we metaphysically draw more individuals into our lives who show up at just the right time to "help" us, and they usually show up with Synchronistic messages and opportunities that protect us and push our lives forward more rapidly. We become literally *luckier*. Life seems easier. Our missions grow clearer.

However, if we take from others—even if we take only energy, unconsciously—then instead of drawing Givers, we draw other *Takers* into our lives who misdirect us and slow down our Synchronicity.

How do we get rid of our unconscious "taking" of energy?

The cure is one of the most discussed processes in the HPM. We can engage in the practice of fully Connecting Spiritually using *Contemplative Meditation*.

In meditation, we seek to let go of the chatter in our minds long enough to find the Experience of our Transcendent, Larger mind that feels like a Connection with a more "knowing," Spiritual part of ourselves.

But as I searched, I found something most people meditating don't seem to know. We can also let go of the "chatter" coming from our emotions and find for ourselves the "Peace that Surpasses All Understanding," suggested by most of the spiritual traditions explored by the HPM.

In this Experience, our hearts open up our Master Emotion: an Agape love—love without an object—that becomes a practiced "state of love." This state, once discovered, establishes our strongest and most stable emotion. After this Experience, whenever we are knocked out of Consciousness by a lower emotion, we can "Come back to Love," and are instantly renewed.

Here, of course, is where we gain our "Inner Security" so often pointed to by the HPM. We no longer need to "defend ourselves" and force energy from others because our Energy Source is unlimited. We can no longer be insulted or lowered by others in the world of fighting for dominance and energy.

We become Energy Givers following The Interpersonal Ethic described in *The Celestine Prophecy*: where becoming a constant energy giver to others becomes a tangible, remembered, habit—where everyone benefits: the other person and ourselves, because as we give, we are filled up with Connected Energy first, as it overflows into others and the world.

And, as you will also remember from *The Celestine Prophecy*, and the other books, there are still other Experiences to expect from our Spiritual Connection.

We open up fully to our "Intuitive Intelligence," where we receive "Guiding Intuitions" that fall into our minds at just the right moment, all suggesting actions to take to stay safe, and bring forth, again, a faster flow of Synchronicity toward our life work.

At this point, I realized the HPM had indeed reached a Synthesis Point, a "Big Picture" revelation about the Spiritual Reality on this Planet. I realized that all this wisdom could go cultural, because our Intuitive Intelligence gives us clues about what other people need as well—allowing our "Giving" to go to another level of effectiveness.

If we tune into our "Intuitive Intelligence," asking, "How might I help this person?" we always get the answer.

It's usually something we have done in our past to solve a problem, or overcome a bad habit, or gain a spiritual breakthrough. And it just comes to mind as an Intuitive thought.

All that's left is to work this Story into the conversation. What do we usually hear from the other person when we share our Intuition? Something like, "Oh my. That's exactly what I needed to hear right now in my life! What a great Synchronicity you gave me!"

Thinking about this, I remember being barely able to keep my feet on the ground! The Spiritual Universe is Designed for each of us to tune in and give Synchronicity to each other in a collective, "High-Speed Flow" to our Missions and Destiny. Most just don't realize the world is Spiritually constructed this way.

What if we could wave a wand and have everyone begin to do this? The world would change dramatically overnight.

Then I remembered the Vision.

It had predicted that I would find this "Big Picture" for the ultimate message of the book.

And again, it was happening right in front of my eyes.

Next was to get clarity about the writing style the book should have. At first, I found myself writing in the academic style most used by the authors I had been reading. And for a while, it seemed to work.

Yet when I had about a hundred pages, I started at the beginning to re-read it and was horrified. It bored me to tears. Something was wrong.

In the Vision, I knew I had figured out how to make the Book interesting—but for now, I was stuck.

And here, at this moment, I went into a sudden, "Dark Night of the Soul."

I had cashed in my retirement account, and it was almost gone. Then unexpected bills threatened to clean it out entirely. I had a car wreck. I got a divorce.

The material world was closing in.

I actually took the manuscript and threw it into a bottom drawer for a while, thinking… well… maybe the kids will find it interesting one day.

Then I concentrated on helping, and when I had enough money, I read Carlos Castaneda's *Journey to Ixtlan* and took off on the road again.

What I found was my Mojo.

Nothing conjures up Synchronicity like a long trek, where people show up at every turn with a bit of wisdom as you go from lost-to-found regularly. Here my engagement with the "Experiences" of the HPM I had read about gradually became Experiential in my life.

The Insights were born. And as I have always said about the Book, it didn't all happen in Peru, but it did happen. I knew at this point that it had to be a full-blown Adventure Story, a parable filled with the characters that could make the Experiences come alive for the readers.

I came home renewed.

A supportive friend called at the very minute I was taking the manuscript out of the drawer to begin writing again. I finished the Book very quickly.

Just when I declared it to be done, my wife Salle arrived, right on time, with her keen eye for detail. "Why aren't there more female characters in this book?" she asked. Oops!

What came next was the last part of the Vision: how to get the Book published and out into the world.

The first thing I remembered from the Vision was that I tested the book before sending it to publishers. I'd never heard of anyone doing this before, but since I had seen it, I figured out that we could test the novel by giving the manuscript to friends of friends, asking for feedback. Over about three months, I gave it to thirty or more people, who each pointed out a place where the book seemed unclear to them, or overwritten, or under-explained.

I treated all the feedback as a big Synchronicity and carefully fixed the problems, until no suggestions were coming in any longer. In fact, we began to receive requests for additional copies, because people wanted to send it to a friend.

And at that point, I knew it was time to approach publishers. In a month or so, we had several offers—only there was a problem. I knew the Book was timely because of the positive feedback, but all the publishers told me it would take two years to get the book into the bookstores.

I was pondering the solution a few days later when an editor friend called and mentioned that she knew a guy locally who was helping people publish their own books.

I smiled. We were going to start our own publishing company.

And that's what we did. We went through the standard ways of designing a book until we had five thousand copies arriving at the door—which resulted in a big increase in Energy, and the sudden memory of what the Vision had showed would be our publicity campaign.

We would give away 1,500 copies.

Our plan was to drive to the twenty largest cities in the US, each of which at the time had at least a dozen large, mom-and-pop bookstores. Because the book was about Synchronicity, and because of our belief in the Karma of giving, we hit the road to the bookstores, offering a Book to each owner or manager as we walked in and explained how they could order more copies.

But in addition, everyone who "happened" to be in the store also got a copy. By the time we returned home, orders were quadrupling every week.

The rest of the Story of *The Celestine Prophecy* is history. We finally turned over the publishing to someone else. The book grew to the top of best-sellers lists across thirty-five countries and stayed there for many years. It continues to be passed around by tens of thousands of new readers every year.

The moral of this Story still stands.

The Universe is designed for our missions to come true, and with our new HPM understanding getting larger, maybe more and more people will embrace their own Visions sooner rather than later.

I still never say that I was chosen to write *The Celestine Prophecy*. But now that I've thought about it, maybe I should consider flipping the issue completely and saying: We Are All Chosen.

So, what are you waiting for? Tune in! Become a Giver! Step into your flow of synchronicity and follow your journey to your special mission!

Yeah. That sounds better!

PS. For anyone who is griping that I didn't give every detail that happened, especially about Peru, I apologize. Not enough room… Besides, you probably wouldn't have believed it anyway.

Blessings to all.

From Disco Queen to Divine Angel
by Sister Dr. Jenna

The coming of God is a coming home to your purity and peace.

Everything was going right for me, at least in terms of wealth... what the world defines as, "it's as good as it gets!" I had fancy clothes, three luxury cars - Mercedes, BMW, and Jaguar, and two nightclubs, one in South Beach, Florida and the other in Key Biscayne. I lived in a modern condo overlooking the Atlantic.

Whenever I entered my nightclubs, people were waiting to see which dress I wore. I was the queen dame, the only young girl running clubs in Miami at that time. I would close the clubs at six a.m. and head to IHOP for pancakes and eggs, then home, going to sleep when the sun was coming up. My awake time was usually around noon and my days would carry on until it was time to head out to the clubs again. I loved life and thought I lived it fully.

I had many ups and downs.

My relationships were fine. I was so focused on myself and what I was creating that I never gave much attention to any one thing or any one person. My focus was on business. Some of my business deals were unsuccessful, and those really hurt—not only because they were financial investments gone bad, but because I was dealing with some of my closest friends at that time. I experienced stress, disappointment, betrayal, and a sense of loss inside my spirit. But it was clouded by all the pomp and show to which I was accustomed.

I was like any young woman, unaware of my future but thinking I was in charge of my destiny. All that I had acquired had come with a great deal of determination, tenacity, and something invisible looking out for me which I could not describe. But there was a turning point when I was heading out one day and I was stressed wondering which car to take. *What am I doing?* I thought.

The blessings of the yogis were upon me.

When I was a teen, my mother started doing meditations at the Brahma Kumaris Center in Miami, Florida. I noticed she was happier, and I started feeling a stronger sense of Divine presence when she was around me. It was magical, like being in the presence of a loving angel. She used to keep sacred texts called the "Murli" around me, and I would read a few lines when she was not around. They were so powerful that they left me amazed.

When I saw my mother being positively and drastically transformed, I became a friend of the Brahma Kumaris, supporting them in whatever way I could. I always knew there was another way to live but becoming a meditation practitioner and spiritual mentor was not in my thoughts. I believed spirituality was great for those who were troubled—but I was fine.

The sisters at the Center were sweet, innocent, and simple—and I was always ready to party. Yet I felt close to them and I liked my interactions with them. They always kept their eyes on me.

On one of my visits to the Center, one of the sisters invited me to stay the weekend. I dismissed the request in my mind and later told my friends what had happened. They said to me, "You want to do meditation? You're going to pollute the place!"

I thought maybe I should give it a try. It was not like I wanted to be a yogi. I was happy with my life. As the weekend approached, I called the Center and told the sisters I would accept their invitation.

On my first morning there, I awakened at four a.m. That is the usual time for yogis to wake up and meditate on inner virtues and take power from the Source. I had never taken interest in any of those things, but there I was, sitting in front of a photo of Brahma Baba, a chariot for the Divine and the founder of the Brahma Kumaris World Spiritual University.

When I looked into his eyes, I started bawling.

I had never cried like that before. It was the first time I felt so vulnerable, yet so protected. I thought it must be the vibrations of the place. There was an unusually good feeling nurturing my soul while I was with the yogis and something was shifting in me.

My friends called to convince me to come back. They told me, "We have this party to go to. Just hurry back." I told them I would come back soon.

At the Center, I had a trance-like experience that would begin to open me up to a whole different world. I felt half-awake, yet I was half-asleep. In the experience, it was as though I was going up an escalator.

At the top, I saw God's energy, calling me: "Come, come, my child." The light was golden and gentle. At the bottom of the escalator, I would hear my friends yelling, "Come, come, what are you doing there!"

It was as if God was saying that he was ready to receive me. I felt the need to go to God but in an instant, the experience vanished, leaving an incredible mark on my soul. When I returned to Miami, I went to my mother and said, "I want to meet God."

I was aware that the Brahma Kumaris had their headquarters at the mountaintop in Mount Abu, Rajasthan in India. Only those who were following the Brahma Kumaris principles of being a vegetarian, following a life of purity, and meditating regularly were usually allowed to go. So my mother, Sister Gita, was shocked I said that. She rejected my request, as I had a totally opposite lifestyle, but I was determined. I asked her to speak with the senior yogis and arrange for me to go to Madhuban, Mount Abu.

Then it happened again: I had another trance-like experience. While on my friend's bike, I had that similar invisible feeling of being protected or guided. We were going at least 100 miles an hour, and I again recalled the experience of God's light calling me. It was powerful! When I reached my condo that day, I learned that Sister Mohini, regional coordinator of the Brahma Kumaris for the Americas and the Caribbean, had given approval for me to go to Madhuban. I had no idea of the profoundly powerful energy I was about to step into.

When I traveled to India for the first time to have my experience of God in Madhuban, I saw thousands of yogis, all dressed in white, who were sweet, calm, and subtly aware of what was going on. I was struck by it all. On one occasion while I was there, I sat a couple of feet away from the stage to experience my meeting with the Divine, through a special instrument named Dadi Gulzar. Her body was used to channel the Divine energy of love, wisdom, purity, and peace. I have heard that her soul's journey has recorded four previous lives of celibacy. When I looked into her eyes, it was clear that there was something beyond the world here.

As Dadi Gulzar was about to invoke the energy of the Divine, I could feel everything I had done in this life that was against my inner truths. They flashed before me like a speeding bullet. Each memory carried its own feeling. The emotion of fear flooded over me, as I sat in front of her, sensing that I was going to experience God but struggling with my past thoughts. Feeling all the different emotions, I was afraid that I would not be able to remain seated, so I started to get up. I wanted to leave the space immediately. As soon as I was ready to run away, the Divine energy entered Dadi's body and looked at me.

God was not interested in my past mistakes.

All my hurtful memories were wiped away within a second. Soaking up the beautiful energy of the space and staring at Dadi, who was channeling the Source of God's love, I sat in my seat for hours. She spoke in Hindi, and although I had English translation available to me, words did not matter. It was like God was rebuilding me from scratch, infusing me with divinity and purity. The person I had been looking at in the mirror for all those years died. I was getting a do-over inside my soul. I stayed in the silent, out-of-this-world experience for the remainder of my visit. This time, the energy was here to stay, no longer to be just a glimpse.

I started to realize that this is God. This is what the world has been talking about. The coming of God was a coming home to your purity and peace, and I was experiencing it!

When I returned to Miami, I was not the same, and I have not touched meat or alcohol since. For a month, I sat in my condo, processing what had happened. Spending time with my mother was comfortable because we now shared a similar experience. We would talk for hours about our experience with the Divine and how we could share it with the world.

Dadi Janki, one of my spiritual mentors in the Brahma Kumaris—who transitioned on March 27, 2020—was visiting the center in Miami a month after I returned from India. She had known me since I was seventeen years old. When I went to meet with her, she looked at me with so much love. She said I was ready. Ready for what? Ready to fly!

The next thing I knew, I was closing my business and heading to New York for spiritual training, under the guidance of Sister Mohini and Sister Kala. Dadi said I could try to live at the Center and see if it worked out. If it did not, I could leave in a couple of months.

Before departing for my new life, my mother took my hand, looked sweetly into my eyes, and said, "Promise me one thing. Never see the defects of another person."

I agreed, and only later realized how powerful her blessing was.

Now in New York at the Ashram, I was amongst seven sisters who had certainly not seen or experienced what I had in my twenty-five years. They were all like angels who walked in silence, prepared and ate food in God's remembrance, and dressed in white.

And here I was, "Jenny from the block"!

Karma Yoga was a powerful practice. I learned that meant that every action was to be performed in God's remembrance, from cooking and cleaning to managing visitors, giving courses, etc. I had to undergo a harsh training because "Jenny from the block" had no idea of the deep, pure energy by which they were being moved. It took me a few years to really surrender into it, and it was and still is the most liberating experience from which one can live.

I chuckle today about an occurrence that took place after a few months in the Ashram. I was asked to draft a letter to invite some influential people to an event. What I thought was the perfect letter came back to me. I was told that it lacked *bhavna*—pure feelings of intent. At the Ashram, I was happy at one level to be in the awakening, but so sad that nothing I did was right. Everything in my energy was wrong. But I knew Dadi Janki does not make mistakes and God does not make mistakes.

I was being taught some deep, sublime ways of how to be true to the self and others. My old self kept fading, and a revised version kept growing. I was being rebuilt every second. There was so much to learn in terms of the manners in which each activity was to be performed—how to speak, walk, sit, eat and be. I felt that the experience of purity was bigger than materialism.

In the disciplined life, I experienced real freedom.

After being in New York for about four years, I was transferred to Washington, D.C. to help set up a center for the Brahma Kumaris. It was then that I realized how much I had learned over the years. God never said that I was defective or broken, or that I was not enough. That was my saving grace.

I have been here now for almost twenty-three years, building the divine presence in Washington, D.C. with two successful museums and our own popular podcast, America Meditating Radio. We are now a powerful, divine force in the region, transmitting our unique vibrations across the nation's capital, and throughout the world.

I transformed from being a disco queen to a divine angel of service. How wonderful is that?

When Spirit Calls
by Judy Lemon

I thank Spirit for pulling me out of a life
that was not the one I came here for.

I stood in shock at the enormous tidal wave that was about to hit me. There was no escape as I felt the turbulent waters of emotion engulf me and take my breath away.

As my consciousness returned, I looked around the room that had been our home office. My husband, Anthony, and I had spent years studying in this room, eventually earning our first degrees together. We had shared so much over the years—but now, staring at the evidence on the screen, I faced a horrible realization on my own: the only man I had ever trusted enough to marry was cheating on me.

The dream life in London that I had manifested slammed abruptly into a wall, taking me along with it.

It was all over.

From an early age, I had wanted to be a professional musician. I took guitar and voice lessons, joined bands, and had a few songs on the local radio, but I wanted more. A teenage fascination with King Arthur and British rock bands led me to London, where I tried my hand at the local music scene.

Along the way, I met Anthony in a pub and we started dating, eventually getting engaged and then married. We had a good life together, traveling throughout Europe and beyond, exploring the English countryside and cooking elaborate meals together on the weekends.

We were both science geeks, and during our walks, we would discuss such topics as quantum physics, electronics, and abstract mathematics. I felt that he was the one man who accepted me for who I was, and I felt safe with him.

Looking back now, I realize that while we could have interesting chats about particle physics and the structure of the universe, we couldn't really talk about us. As the years passed, I began to feel that we were trapped in eternal adolescence.

Where were we really going?

Anthony worked in the computing field and was vehemently against even looking at a computer when he got home from work. But after a weekend trip to another country, he suddenly seemed to be very interested in computer work in the evenings. He'd go into the back room and close the door, claiming to be working on some important project from home.

My intuition left me unsettled; something wasn't as it appeared to be. One day while he was at work, I turned on our shared computer and poked around a bit. On the surface, nothing seemed out of order, but I was suddenly guided to look at the history tab and discovered that he had a secret email account. I felt my heart stop.

Over the next few days, I managed to hack into his account and saw that he had met a woman during our weekend vacation. In the few short hours that he'd nipped down to the hotel bar, he'd picked up a local woman and was now carrying on a long-distance affair with her. It was this evidence that had slammed into me like a shock wave.

I remained silent for many months as I gathered evidence and tried to figure out how best to handle the situation. I monitored their communications and tried to keep a straight face when he'd lie about his whereabouts. He'd bring his girlfriend to London, paying for her expenses out of our household bank account. He'd put her up in a hotel and then tell me he was meeting with work colleagues or some other nonsense like that.

He didn't know I'd also found a box that he'd hidden in his closet that had photos of them together, poetry they'd written to each other, and all sorts of letters. The one man I'd trusted turned out to be just like all the others I'd been with over the years.

I eventually confronted him and asked for a divorce.

He continued to see her, leaving airline tickets in plain view or calling her while I was at home. I didn't know why he was taunting me, since he was the one who had strayed. I felt he should move out, but he refused, so I did.

I knew someone who lived across town in a crummy area of London's east end. Gil was a Tarot reader at an esoteric shop in Covent Garden, and I'd taken a series of classes on ceremonial *magick* with him. Along with other students, we'd go out after class and engage in lively discussions over a few pints before heading to our respective homes.

Gil had a two-bedroom council flat and offered me a refuge from the hell that my marriage had become. I accepted and spent weeks carefully boxing up my possessions, not sure when they'd see the light of day again.

I would load up the car with whatever would fit, drive through London, and haul everything into Gil's council house. Once I had everything in place, I brought over our three cats, since Anthony no longer wanted anything to do with them.

While I knew that living with Gil wasn't going to be wonderful, my hope was that I'd be able to rebuild my life in London and continue to pursue my musical dreams. But as it turned out, the real hell was about to begin.

Walking with the Witch Master.

My path to the magical arts had started a few years prior when I learned to meditate. As I immersed myself in the practices, I began to hear the voice of my higher self and wanted to dive in much deeper. When I saw an ad in the *London Standard* for a course on ceremonial magick taught by a male Witch, I just had to be a part of it. That course led to an exploration of other magical subjects such as witchcraft, the Wicca religion, and eventually shamanism. After a week in a remote camp in North Wales learning about shamanism, I felt like this was something I could relate to and really make my own. Shamanism became my lifeline.

I had wanted to share these interests with Anthony. He had learned to meditate so we could go on weekend retreats together, but it wasn't long before he returned to find his spirit in a bottle instead of within himself. Having been brought up with no discernible religion or spiritual practices, he couldn't understand my interest in such strange practices.

I believe that the day I learned to meditate was the beginning of the end of our marriage.

Once I had settled into Gil's crummy council flat, his true character began to emerge. He had been doted on by a mother who died when he was in his twenties, so I felt he was looking for another woman to take care of him. When I didn't give him the attention he was constantly seeking, he became like a little boy on the edge of a tantrum. Threatening to kick me out, he would start hauling my stuff out into the hall to "reclaim his space." I would then have to immediately deal with whatever outburst he was having, to keep my possessions from being carried away by the local hoodlums.

I couldn't return to my nice flat in the West End because my soon-to-be ex-husband was flaunting his girlfriend quite openly now. I felt trapped and began to drink myself into numbness daily, as soon as I woke up. I knew what I was doing wasn't good for me, but I no longer cared. Maybe I could just drink myself to death to end this hideous nightmare.

During one of these binges, my three cats wandered into the room and looked at me. Samrat, the male, was the ringleader of this feline trio and he gazed at me with his wise, green eyes. He seemed to know what I was thinking.

A curious feeling came over me as I looked at the three cats that had been with me in happier times and were now in hell with me. How could I leave them? They had brought me so much solace that I couldn't imagine leaving them to an uncertain fate if I left the world. In that moment, I made a promise to them.

"While you guys are in your physical bodies, I will be here for you. The four of us will stay together and get through this somehow."

I began to see that my life in London was over.

During one phone conversation with my parents, my mother said that I was welcome to come home and start my life over if I wanted to. I told her I would consider this, but I really did not want to return to the United States. I loved London and being so close to Europe, and the idea of moving back in with my parents in my forties made me feel like a real loser.

My mother and I had never had a close relationship, and when I was growing up, we were always at each other's throats. The idea of being back in the same house that I'd grown up in and where I'd endured so many battles and backhanders did not appeal to me, but I had nowhere else to go. Having reached rock bottom, I decided to return to the States with my three cats and face whatever was in store for me.

I had hoped that with the passing of the years that my relationship with my mother would be more peaceful, but it was not. It was as if we'd picked up right where we'd left off twenty years earlier and added more force and volume. I'd gone from living with a lying cheater, to a lunatic wizard, and then back to the screaming matches of my adolescence. Little did I know, this was where my life started to shift from mayhem to miracles.

I looked for every excuse to get out of the house and away from my mother and her moods, so I went back to school and got a degree in forensics. I also took every Spanish class the school offered, as well as other courses in indigenous studies. While I thought lifting fingerprints off cadavers was kind of cool, I realized I wasn't a police person. The voices of shamanism and plant spirits became louder, and I began to look around for groups where I could develop my interests in these areas.

My divorce settlement was delayed four years because I had moved back to the States, Anthony had moved to his girlfriend's home country, and both sets of lawyers were in London. The waiting was truly awful. I was penniless when I moved back home and didn't like the feeling that anyone had power over me, after living a life of luxury in London's West End for so many years. But as soon as my money came through, I felt free to fly. Not long after that, I followed my instinct to go on a plant spirit medicine retreat in Peru, and my life took a drastic turn when I met the medicine man who became my first teacher.

The work of the shamanic apprentice is more than ceremony.

It also involves a lot of painful introspection and healing of one's own soul. During the many years I continued to face my shadow side, my relationship with my mother changed. As I healed, the higher vibrations rippled outwards to my family members and the shouting matches ceased. The most astonishing thing that happened was that, before my mother died, I was able to tell her that I loved her, and I meant it. To this day, this gives me great peace.

When we are at the bottom of our pits of despair, it's hard to see a way out. It's only later, sometimes many years later, that we can look back and see why we had to go through what we did. I had a task to perform in this life that, for some reason, I couldn't fulfill in London with Anthony.

And those three dear cats fulfilled their own life missions of keeping me alive until I could be healed and on my way. I was with each of them as they passed into the spirit world, thanking them for their unbounded love and support.

Every day, I thank Spirit for pulling me out of a life that was not the one I came here for. Through all that madness and mayhem, I have become the healer and the spiritual teacher that I was born to be. This is a true miracle.

The Miracle of Finding Your Voice
by Laura Rowley

Listening to animals' voices, I finally learned to trust my own.

I exhaled with exhaustion, having completed my last consultation with the horse named Cara. Cara, a successful show horse, had excelled at her job as a show jumper. Now, suddenly, Cara refused to enter the arena. She scattered horses, people, and officials as she flung herself away from the gate and into the crowd.

Her owner, Jenn, had booked an appointment with me to explore the performance breakdown currently dominating their relationship. Jenn had tried her best skills as a horsewoman to avoid harming others. She was embarrassed at her sudden fall from grace and scared that something was seriously amiss with her beloved Cara.

As a professional animal communicator, it's a privilege helping animals and their people get back on track. When Jenn called, I immediately tuned into Cara and listened to her side of the story. Fortunately, Cara was an eloquent communicator herself, showing me a series of images and emotions that were coursing through her. I relayed those ideas to Jenn, who was surprised by some, while recognizing others.

195

Cara felt a sharp pain in her leg. She had protected herself by avoiding the ten jumps that awaited her, had she entered the ring. She hoped Jenn would give special notice to her crazy behavior, because Cara knew she was injured. Jenn would confirm this several days later, after her vet used an ultrasound machine to diagnose a tear in a major tendon in Cara's front leg. These small tears can turn into catastrophic injuries upon landing off a jump.

Cara had felt the sudden pain erupt after her last practice jump, moments before she refused to enter the arena. A consummate professional athlete, Cara knew she could not continue, to protect herself and Jenn. Her refusal to perform was a signal to Jenn, though she hated being disobedient.

Jenn had a lot to process in our joint conversation with Cara.

Jenn felt guilt and embarrassment for her own lack of understanding. She had nearly forced her horse to perform and ultimately could have injured her. Jenn said she'd had a strong intuition that Cara wasn't completely comfortable earlier that day, but she had chosen to ignore it. Cara moved athletically, so her owner was able to dismiss her sense that something wasn't right.

Cara generously reaffirmed her love of Jenn, as animals understand far better than we humans that mistakes happen and it's the love that really counts. Jenn was moved to tears, and I was left profoundly grateful to help them reach an understanding. Jenn apologized to Cara, who forgave easily.

Tired as I felt, I reflected that our world would be peaceful if all misunderstandings could be worked through so beautifully. I felt deep gratitude for the vulnerability both Jenn and Cara had displayed, reminding me that love heals all. I could have kissed the universe for giving me this place of professionally working by using my intuition.

I often marvel that I got here at all.

I entered adulthood, like most people, guided by unexamined fears. What if I didn't get where I was supposed to go? That could have been the title of my first three decades of life. It was my guiding principle for a lot of my major decisions. I felt a deep calling, without understanding what was calling me. I felt odd; my fellow college students studied and entered their professions, while I had the sensation I was in training for something that I hadn't yet met.

I completed my bachelor's degree in philosophy and literature but continued to work in sales for my family's construction company. I knew my career and marriage needed serious amendments or reconsiderations, but I was afraid to explore my unhappiness. I remember thinking that if I knew what I wanted, then I could make changes accordingly.

My family believed in keeping a stiff upper lip. Perseverance and toughness were the hallmarks of success. My charismatic father had lost his father at the age of twelve, spinning him into a harsh reality where family priorities meant work, not education. He became a union bricklayers' apprentice, and through hard work, came to own a 200-employee construction company. Our family legend had the deep ethnos that if you struggled, you could ultimately triumph. Never mind that the work might be difficult, lonely, and sometimes unbearable; these emotions could be pushed down. It was better to rely on your willpower for success.

Our family life swirled around the demands created by my father's career and cardiac illness. We were helpmates to my stressed, beleaguered mother. "Let's not upset Dad" was the resounding refrain I'd heard since first grade. I became acutely watchful of my parent's needs and tried to be a good girl, while our family spent all its energy on not feeling emotions. In his mid-fifties, after multiple heart attacks, my father left my family to join another. My heartbroken mother never recovered from this blow. They both passed away in their late fifties, leaving a wide swath of painful, unfinished emotional trauma for their three daughters.

At thirty-four, I needed to address the crippling pattern of putting another's emotional needs before my own. Mistakenly thinking suffering would bear fruit, I endured through life challenges, fearing change.

It finally occurred to me that I deserved happiness.

I was a physical and emotional wreck. Asthma, allergies, and insomnia are the physical manifestations of a person who isn't taking care of herself on the most fundamental level... self-love. I was swept up by a desire to reclaim myself. I told my eldest sister, "I can sense a train coming down the tracks and I know I should get out of the way, but I am going to let it take my life apart." I didn't know it then, but the train I felt was the wall of buried emotions that erupted wildly, refusing to honor logic.

I ended my twelve-year marriage gracelessly, causing pain I didn't intend but felt helpless to prevent. My career shifted radically to working with horses professionally, managing a training barn—and then I moved to the South, remarried, and started breeding horses. My wounded ego was full of self-recrimination: "I should have known better."

I started meditating and found myself drawn to the great writers who studied subtle energy bodies. I'd read and reflect that I almost knew the information with a kind of precognition. Difficult spiritual subjects felt more like forgotten memories, leaving me vaguely tingly and eager to study further.

When my sister invited me on a spiritual retreat to Scotland, I did not hesitate. As we discussed esoteric ideas and prayed in ancient cathedrals, I experienced dreams and precognitions filled with hope. One morning, I paused to enjoy the Scottish countryside's sweeping views as a woman marched up. I had a clear thought that her right knee hurt, because the energy around it looked dark. When I blinked and looked again, there was no energy in evidence, and I doubted my peculiar intuition.

Then she said, "Mind if I rest here? My knee is killing me!"

I surprised myself by saying that I'd thought as much. In the past, I would have edited my response, since it might have seemed inappropriate. My unfiltered self was emerging. The woman smiled and said, "Ancient sacred sites like cathedrals often have unusual effects on people, because they elevate us."

Had she scoffed or laughed, my ego would have felt foolish and I might have faltered into skepticism. Faith in my own intuition was starting to be a requirement if I were to grow. This was an enormous breakthrough, connecting me to Source energy directly.

Upon returning to the US, I was doing my daily barn chores one day. As I rolled up the water hose, I distinctly heard a voice say, "Hey, I'm thirsty." I wandered down the aisle, glancing into each of the five horse stalls and wondering what I'd heard. Lump occupied the last stall. I noticed his empty bucket. He didn't pause in his hay chewing when I asked if he'd spoken.

I filled his bucket while he gulped the water thirstily. Later, when I joined my husband, I told him of my insight. I half expected him to laugh, but he causally looked up and said, "You probably did hear him" ...as if talking to animals was normal for me!

I redoubled my daily meditation practice, caught up and confused by these voices I heard. I stood under an oak tree and felt anxieties slip into a deep calm. There, I acquainted myself with spiritual wisdom, awash with a gratitude for everything, including my confusion.

We all have the gift of intuition.

It is an inner knowing about how we can be our best, and therefore do our best, in the world. What we care about and love in life feeds our souls, allowing self-discovery to morph into self-love. My natural talents of empathy grew, and I astonished myself, hearing animals' voices increasingly. Could I trust this? Trust myself?

During this time, a veterinarian working on our horses shared her distress. Her elderly Husky had retreated under her bed for days. I had the clearest vision and blurted out, "Her liver is swollen." The vet arched her eyebrow, saying the ultrasound of the previous week was normal. I was embarrassed until she phoned me the next day. "I retook the ultrasound, and the dog's liver *is* swollen. How did you know that?" she said.

At that point, I knew I'd better start trusting Spirit.

Since childhood, I'd learned to anticipate my parents' unvoiced needs, a pattern that wasn't healthy because I excluded my own. I was always un-present in my own life and busy in the life of others. My extreme love of animals and a desire to see them well and happy, followed with reverence, led me to my natural talents of being highly intuitive with them. My empathy, once honored, proved an amazing guidance system into a career of twenty-five years helping others understand their animals, and even themselves. I have done sessions with more than 60,000 animals. Each feels like a mini miracle.

Animals seek out such vibrations; they are drawn to what feels good, because it is part of their survival mechanism. But much more than that, they tell me in nearly every session that they love to be with us when we are throbbing with love and joy. Animals thrive, people strive. We allow our egos and our minds to carry us in an endless loop of planning. We fret about what, where, and why. Animals do what feels better. They wonder why we don't behave that way. They feel dismay when we fall off our own happy bandwagon, seeking to right us when we wobble.

Recently, Ralph, an elderly Labrador Retriever, asked his owner, "Why are you always frowning and grinding your teeth when you sit in your office?" His owner glibly replied, "It's how I pay our bills so you can have lots of toys."

Next, she started crying when Ralph responded, "I'd rather have you smiling on the inside."

I now see how my upbringing was perfect. I learned how easily people, my current and past clients, lose themselves in doing what seems hard rather than joyful. Animals who love us notice this energetic disparity in their human family…they nudge us toward greater self-awareness. They long for us to join them in relaxation, playing and loving. They invite us into gentleness, saying yes and allowing love.

I rejoice that, in listening to animals' voices, I finally learned to trust my own.

An Alcoholic's Progression from Mayhem to Miracles

by Sharla Charpentier

I finally put myself and my well-being first.
And that's when the miracles started happening.

My childhood was full of codependency. I took it upon myself to make sure everyone else had their needs met as I played my role of the "good daughter."

The mayhem in my life began in middle school when I took my first drink.

I discovered intoxication allowed me to finally let go of my inhibitions and be my true self. Drinking relieved my constant, underlying anxiety and boosted my low self-esteem. Despite my "partying" as a young adult, I was able to hold it together—or so it appeared. People perceived me as outgoing, confident, ambitious, and successful. I continued to be the good daughter, good family member, good student, good girlfriend, good friend, and good employee.

But I had lost sight of my own goals and made choices for other people rather than for myself. I felt pressured to go to law school, despite my college professor warning me that my personality did not fit the law student/lawyer profile. My gut instinct told me law school was not the right path for me, but I didn't listen. I was always creative, but creativity was not what those around me wanted me to pursue.

So, despite my reservations, I convinced myself law school made sense. It was the practical thing successful people do. Soon after graduating from law school, I got married, although I knew deep down that this was also a wrong decision. I gave up my own goals and dreams to help someone else achieve theirs.

I had no clue what I wanted to do or what was aligned with my soul. I had spent so much of my life drinking and not thinking about myself that I was completely out of touch with my spiritual side.

Resentment followed, and the mayhem continued.

I started having children soon after getting married, because that's what society at that time dictated for women of my age to do. My four children are absolute blessings and miracles, but at the time, I was unable to appreciate their births because I suffered from postpartum depression after each delivery. Undiagnosed and not medically treated after my first baby's birth for nearly a year, I was deeply depressed and felt lost and alone. With each child, I gave up more and more of my own identity.

At this point in my life, I was incapable of taking care of myself. All of my energy went to my children and marriage. They came first, no matter what the cost. I worked through each pregnancy at a job I didn't identify with, nursed each baby while completely sleep-deprived, and tried to manage my growing family with the majority of household responsibilities resting on my shoulders. I agreed to move back to a state where my husband could have his dream job without considering where I wanted to live or what made me happy.

My interests were never my first priority. I was only comfortable taking care of others, never myself. Throughout all these years, I was self-medicating with alcohol more and more, not realizing I was also struggling with bipolarism. The resentment I felt grew, and the mayhem of my life progressed.

I got divorced, fell apart, and used alcohol "to survive." My bipolarism advanced during this time and I became more unstable. At thirty-eight, divorced, living in a state without any family, with four kids relying on me, working endless hours, I had no clue how to take care of myself in a healthy manner.

I was broken physically, mentally, emotionally, and spiritually; my life was complete mayhem.

By the grace of God, I did not kill myself or anyone else from drunk driving. I did not get arrested or lose custody of my children or lose my job. But I did lose myself. I lost my identity, my spirit, and my self-worth. Aside from my children, any hope, faith, joy, and peace that I ever had in my life were gone. I finally realized that something had to change—not for myself (not yet) but for my children.

After drinking all night and passing out in the early morning, I woke up midday completely hungover on my fortieth birthday. My parents were visiting from out of state, and my kids were waiting for me to open their presents. While I opened their gifts, I felt physically ill.

While my kids and parents ate my birthday cake that I myself could not eat, I finally put myself first. I admitted that I was an alcoholic and could not and never would be able to drink "normally." For my birthday, I was given the greatest of gifts—desperation—and I surrendered.

My first step toward saving myself and stopping the mayhem was walking through the doors of a 12-Step program.

This program gave me the tools I needed to save myself, as well as the blessing of self-recovery. I continued to put myself first, saw a therapist for my codependency issues, figured out the correct medication for my bipolarism, and worked the 12 Steps.

I started discovering myself again, and the miracles began.

I remembered what I had enjoyed as a child and reflected on what made me happy, not what fit the "good daughter/good wife" mold. Writing poems helped me tap into my creative side, where I found serenity and peace—a miracle.

I reconnected with my cousin/soul sister, who was also dual-diagnosed as a bipolar alcoholic and who had been appropriately medicated and sober for several years. We had walked almost identical paths, and we now shared the same dreams. We decided to make our dreams of writing educational and adventurous children's books come true.

I now put myself first, and it works. After more than twenty-five years of drinking, my life is full of miracles. I am sober now for more than three years and am content with my life as it is. I am fully present with my children and cherish my time with them. I have good relationships with family members. I co-parent with my ex-husband in a healthy manner. I have close friends that I can trust. I have fun without drinking.

It is a miracle that I am a published author of a children's book series, and that I am part of the artistic process of this same children's book series with my original character sketches. It is a miracle that I can help others by sharing my story of mayhem to miracles. It is a miracle that I love myself. So many miracles in one lifetime; I am truly blessed.

My life is no longer a progression of mayhem, but a progression of miracles.

I honestly believe that, if I am true to myself and put my well-being first, the miracles are endless. There are miracles all around me every day. I was born a miracle. Each day, I can wake up and choose to see miracles in my life. And each day hereafter, I will grab onto those miracles and never let go.

Finding the Words to Change My Life
by Jill Ammon Vanderwood

A miracle was beginning to happen in my life.

When I was ten years old, our family moved from a rural Oregon town to the city of Portland. We camped all summer, because it took so long for my dad to find a job and for my parents to find a place to live. When we finally moved into a home, we couldn't afford to pay the moving company's storage fees to reclaim our personal belongings.

Our large family moved into an empty house with no furniture and no school clothes, shoes, or school supplies. My mother was expecting her tenth baby in September, so my parent's focus was on making my mother comfortable and bringing my little brother into the world. We relied on neighbors and people from our church to supply the hand-me-down clothes we would need to attend school.

I started the fifth grade at a school where all the other students knew each other. I felt very awkward there, where everything from the games they played to the level of learning was so different. I'm pretty sure I dressed differently than most of the kids, and without even trying, I stood out from others.

That was also the year that my teacher had a baby, so in the middle of the year, she went on leave and we had a whole series of substitute teachers who didn't even know what was going on in the classroom. One boy had been bullying the others in the class. Ray was taller and bigger than most of the other boys, so they blindly followed whatever he told them. Ray just happened to notice me, and he got the other boys in class to start bullying me.

I was laughed at, spit at, tripped, and called hurtful names.

It was hard for me to go to school, because I was bullied every day by the boys in my school room. I'm sure most of my class didn't even know why I was the target that year. One of the boys who had been in the class told me, years later, that he was so glad when Ray stopped bullying him that he went along with whatever Ray asked him to do.

One event that stands out to me the most was when all the girls in my class stood up for me by choosing me to run for class president. And I won! In the backlash of hate from the fifth-grade boys, I quickly resigned.

That same year, each class member was assigned a topic, and we needed to take turns giving oral reports. I didn't wear the right outfit that day. My skirt was too tight around the waist, so I unbuttoned the top button when I sat down at my desk. When my teacher called my name, I stood up and my skirt fell all the way to the floor. At least I was wearing a slip, so my underwear didn't show! I quickly pulled my skirt up and walked to the front of the class. Red-faced, I looked around to see who was laughing. I knew I couldn't give a report if the whole class had seen my skirt fall. It was as if time stood still.

These two incidents are indelible in my memory.

I'm certain that my extreme fear of public speaking began in the fifth grade. Before that, I'd performed ballet in front of an audience, and I was a member of a harmonica band. School days can be cruel for kids, and the bullying I endured that year left me without the courage to perform. I just wanted to fade into the background.

By the next year, my sister was also being bullied. We tried to tell our parents about these pests, but our dad said, "just be nice to them and they will leave you alone." But how could we be nice to these bullies? What my sister and I learned from that exchange was that we were alone in this, so why even bother telling our parents?

I also had bad teeth.

On top of the problem, I had with the bullies, I also had bad teeth, which made me want to hide my mouth when I talked. I would never talk to anyone without putting a hand in front of my mouth. By the time I was in the eighth grade, my teeth had gotten worse.

I was still trying to blend in and never call any attention to myself when, after a prolonged illness, my hair began to fall out in handfuls. I started high school with long, stringy hair that wouldn't cover my ears, even when I pulled all my hair forward.

I ate lunch with my best friend, who also wanted to eat with her new friends. I went along with it until one day, while using the bathroom, I overheard her friend say, "Keep Jill in the bathroom for a little while, because I'm meeting up with my boyfriend. I don't want him to think I go around with her."

I ran past her, out of the bathroom, and said, "Who'd want to be friends with you, anyway!"

Life just kept sneaking up on me and my confidence continued to suffer.

I was shy and withdrawn, never talking to people unless I felt comfortable around them. In class, I wouldn't raise my hand or speak up, even though I had so much to say. I usually walked to school alone.

By the tenth grade, my hair began to grow back. When I was in the eleventh grade, I finally had my teeth fixed, but the damage to my self-image wasn't so easy to repair. Because of my problems with communication, I started to write down my thoughts. I also read books and kept journals. My self-consciousness continued for many years.

I got married when I was nineteen and had three children within the first three years. Although I didn't realize it, I was developing my writing skills while my children were young by making up songs that we sang together. When I had grandchildren, I wrote poems and stories that included my grandchildren as main characters.

A miracle was beginning to happen in my life.

My writing started to change me. While writing my first children's book, in my fifties, I joined the League of Utah Writers and started entering my nonfiction stories into contests. I would sit in the audience at award ceremonies and say over and over to myself, "Please don't win! Please, please don't win!" because I was terrified to stand up in front of a crowd and read my piece. As I kept entering contests, a funny thing began to happen—I started winning!

Two of my writer friends and I decided to take a community education class on public speaking. In that class, we all had to stand up and introduce ourselves. That was so scary for me. At the end of the class, the teacher told me that, out of her whole class, I was the most scared.

When my first book was published, I became the president of my local writer's chapter. I also contacted the head of the statewide group to volunteer to teach a workshop on marketing at the annual conference. Now I had six months to figure out what I was going to do. How could I get up in front of a group of more experienced writers to teach a workshop? I said many prayers asking God to give me the strength and courage I needed.

That is when I joined Toastmasters. I was certainly afraid of giving speeches, but the first speeches were only three minutes, and I had the advantage of being able to write the speeches. You don't go to a Toastmaster's meeting without being involved. You need to schedule ten speeches that help you learn certain things, like hand gestures and using props and graphs, etc. Before long, I was winning blue ribbons for my short speeches and helping out as a timer, or "ah master"—the person who writes down how many times a speaker says "um" or "ah" in their speech.

When the day came for me to teach the workshop for the League of Utah Writers, I spoke to other presenters who were giving workshops. Several people told me that there were only two people in their workshop. I thought, oh, this is great! I will have my sister-in-law and my friend there, and they will be my two people. This will be easy.

Before I taught my workshop, I took an allergy pill to get rid of the frog in my throat. I had all my notes and props ready. But then it happened. The room began to fill up! All the seats in the room were full, and people were standing along the sides! I lost my place in my notes!

My mouth was so dry from the allergy pill that my lips stuck to my teeth, then I lost all of my notes onto the floor. But I kept talking.

I had no idea how it went, and I really didn't care at that point, because I did it! I stood there for nearly an hour with a room full of people and I finished my workshop. An experienced writer came up to me afterward and said, "You seemed a little scared at first, but after you warmed up, you gave some great information and really did well."

That was a breakthrough for me!

Since that day, I have taught many more writer's workshops and published many more books. When my anthology *Shaking Behind the Microphone, Overcoming the Fear of Public Speaking* was published, I was asked to give a keynote speech for the League of Utah Writers. I spoke on overcoming the fear of public speaking during the lunchtime session. And I did it!

After *Erase the Problem of Bullying* was published, I was asked to appear on a New York TV program as a bullying expert during the 2016 election campaign.

Sometimes my old fears and doubts begin to creep in, but I trust in God that I will have the right words to say and that He will help me to say them. My fear disappears, and I quickly find the words. And by the way, I never speak using notes, just in case I lose my place—I only use bullet points.

A Significant Fork
by Mehdi Bouneb

One path illuminated itself while the other remained in the dark.

How did I get to this point?

I hit the ground hard. I didn't know where I was, but I could tell this space was much darker than anything I'd experienced in my twenty-six years. I was hurting and felt supremely alone.

It was noon and I was ready to leave the famed Spearmint Rhino, where I'd spent the previous six hours blankly conversing with exotic dancers while snorting a mountain of cocaine in the bathroom. This hard-hitting fall was the perfect culmination to a month-long binge.

As I walked out into the sun's scorching light, I sensed my soul hiss like a vampire and knew I needed to cloak myself with the darkness of my bedroom. But considering the copious amounts of drugs in my system, this seemed like a far-fetched possibility.

On the cab ride home, which felt like my longest walk of shame ever, I began to question my entire life. *What's the point anymore? Is there one?* If there was, I knew I was blowing right past it.

The card I never thought I'd draw had now become my reality. Rock bottom was inevitable.

Alone at home and recovering by my pool from the crushing weekend, I had no choice but to face the gravity of my current state. I could no longer hide in the safety of my own shadow.

On this lonely avenue, I knew my mind, body, heart, and soul had gotten numb to the point where I'd lost every part of myself. Even my addictions to marijuana, cocaine, LSD, MDMA, and nicotine—or "my girls," as I like to call them—could no longer provide me with any sort of solace in my pathetic existence. In my mind, all I needed now was something to push me over the edge and into the pit of eternal death. After all, what man desires to live high daily? Why would this man choose to torture himself this way?

As of that moment, I had nothing driving me forward and nothing tying me to the past. Ready to leave this world behind, I knew what I had to do.

"Yo… I'm coming to pick up heroin," I texted one of my dealers. "See you soon."

Once I'd gotten into my car, I turned on the engine, only to simultaneously start sobbing. With tears running down both sides of my face, my eyes blinded by a teary cloud, I put my hands on the steering wheel and braced myself for the road ahead.

But I just froze.

How did it get this bad?

Suddenly, I heard a voice in my head, repeating the following: "Go down this road if you wish, but know that you'll never make it out alive. It'll be the end of you."

My sliver of light, not yet ready to be claimed by the darkness, was tightly clinging to dear life.

Over the course of the next hour, I debated whether to make the four-hour drive to Los Angeles or stay home. Having done synthetic opium in the past, smoked heroin in college, and taken Oxycontin for a week, I knew that daily opioid use would bring a sad conclusion to my existence. I was ready to end it all.

In my hesitation, I found myself at a fork in the road.

Faced with two options, one path illuminated itself while the other remained in the dark.

On this bright road, I had alienated myself from anyone I could call a friend. I had also disowned my family, not wanting to pull them into my shallow storm. I was walking down the loneliest avenue. With nothing to live for and no one to turn to, I could take enough heroin to overdose and allow my heart to flatline, alone at home. Nobody would've known.

Did that mean the darkened way led to a sober life?

The choice was mine – should I head down the path of my impending death or could I use today as the catalyst to start living a sober life? I wanted to be sober, but I just didn't know if I was strong enough to say goodbye to my girls.

My first drops of alcohol, eleven years earlier, had led me to this point. It had started as a seemingly innocent progression. Casual beers became the norm for my friends and me, and upon starting high school, we graduated to hard liquor. With my inhibitions lowered, I'd discovered a gateway to an exciting new world. From there, saying yes to new experiences became easier than taking candy from a baby.

I smoked my first joint at seventeen, and so began the "let's get stoned" era. Puffing and laughing with my homies on our local park bench was my favorite way to kill time after school.

The following year, I leaped forward into a dance with heroin-based ecstasy. Endless energy, pure bliss, and enveloping comfort. Who knew you could take a pill and dance the night away to beautiful music? I certainly didn't. What a thrill!

A year after the wildest night of my life, I had my first tryst with cocaine in the foul-smelling bathroom of an underground nightclub in Zurich. Deep tech-house and cocaine? It was a match made in heaven. The odor of vomit quickly faded as the bitter cocaine made herself comfortable in my nostrils and intense euphoria settled in. Later that night, in a shady strip club bathroom, my face went numb and I landed on Cloud Nine.

All I wanted was to experience the fun side of adolescence. But when I moved to Manchester, England to pursue my bachelor's degree, I realized how much I yearned for everything I'd tried up to this point. As a result, my college life consisted of four years of heavy drinking, weekly stay-at-home nights with marijuana, social smoking at nightclubs, and the occasional waltz with MDMA.

Once I graduated from college, I moved to the City of Angels, where I scored a media-sales internship. Despite working five days a week, nightfall was when I ultimately started soaring through the clouds.

By this point, alcohol was no longer my headliner. I now had a taste of the finer things in life and was spending quality time with Mary Jane (marijuana), Coco (cocaine), Molly (MDMA), and Nikki (nicotine). Bottle service at the clubs became the standard, and afterparties in the

Hollywood Hills meant I was high until sunrise. All I needed was to know the right people and all my needs were taken care of.

During my second trip to Las Vegas since my arrival in Los Angeles, I discovered an environment where my partying ways could reach new heights. After a wild forty-eight hours, I drove back to Los Angeles feeling magnetized by Sin City's opulent club scene. The last of my inhibitions faded quicker than the glittering lights in my rearview mirror. Catching myself grinning like a Cheshire cat, I knew the city had dug its claws into my heart and it was only a matter of time before this oasis in the middle of the desert became my home.

One hot July night, I bought my first seven grams of psilocybin mushrooms. As I hadn't a clue what to expect from a psychedelic substance, I started with two grams, by myself. Over the course of six hours, I'd learned that eating mushrooms was like nothing I'd experienced before. It cracked open a door inside of me. I felt grounded and connected to the earth, and this led me to ask questions I'd never thought to ask.

Who is Mehdi Bouneb? What's my purpose in life? What's the meaning of life? What do I want? Where do I come from? Why am I here?

Because I hadn't the faintest idea how to answer these questions, I allowed myself to further venture down the rabbit hole and make myself at home. My next fix became my only priority. I dropped out of a master's degree program and chose to move to San Diego, California, where I became a full-time slave to my addictions.

I never truly understood why I abused drugs this way, but I always wanted to do something out of the ordinary—something weird and crazy.

Sobriety.

But can that even be possible, given that I was powerless in the face of my girls?

When I started to research success stories from former addicts, I realized that traditional rehab could be an option, but I was quickly deterred by the expense. I needed another way.

Through my research, I stumbled upon plant medicine retreats in Costa Rica. Curious, I studied the plant ayahuasca in detail.

While ayahuasca shouldn't be viewed as a miracle cure, this medicine seemed to have the ability to help with post-traumatic stress disorder, depression, drug addiction, and other mental, physical, and spiritual traumas. Ayahuasca could be used as a tool for learning from past experiences, gaining new perspectives, and creating positive change.

After I'd reviewed all the information, I decided to give this alternate medicine a shot. I attended my first medicine retreat, free from expectations. The retreat was on a vast piece of land and offered private bedrooms with *en suite* bathrooms, daily cooked meals from the in-house chef, a pool and hot tub, and stunning views of the Nicoya peninsula from the backyard. The retreat center had a vibe of a comfortable sanctuary for peace, healing, and relaxation.

After two introductory ceremonies, I was given a platform to start educating myself—and that was when I started to write my second book. Was I healed from my addictions? No, but I felt that by feeding my passion, writing, I could eventually get to a sober point. I just had to believe I could.

When I broke my promise to myself to remain sober after my first retreat, I knew that my journey with drugs was far from over.

I had learned a lot about myself my first time around with the plant medicine, but I also knew that ayahuasca isn't something that will heal you with the snap of a finger. Getting what you want from the medicine is a process.

Consequently, I decided to take part in a second retreat to continue learning and peel away more layers to my addictions. In reality, I never should have attended this retreat. Your body should be clear of all substances prior to drinking ayahuasca. Failing to observe this rule can be fatal. Knowingly, I put my life in danger by consuming excessive amounts of drugs for seven days prior to my first ceremony. I was reckless, completely disregarding my preparation and my life, for that matter. In my mind, I just wanted to die. Luckily, I came home unharmed, and within five days, I had another relapse.

At this point, I asked myself: *Can ayahuasca actually help me?*

I truly had no idea, so I decided to not take part in any more retreats. With all hope lost, I unleashed a crushing, four-month binge that culminated with a hard-hitting bang.

After opening my eyes to the state I had reached, I sat in my car as I contemplated my next move: either I start using heroin and slowly kill myself, or I just try my hardest to get sober.

Once I'd debated whether I should make the drive to Los Angeles or stay home, I turned off the engine and messaged my dealer to let him know I wouldn't be coming. There were no hard feelings—just a message wishing me luck.

At rock bottom, I made the conscious decision to release the need for all substances. And although I was shaking all the way down to my core, I stepped onto the darkened path with uncertainty ahead. It was time to flip the script, grow up, and put my life back together.

Through my own doing, my friends were out of reach. If I continued down this self-destructive road, I'd end up losing everything else. There was no time to dwell on the past, but I could write a better future by living sober. It was about damn time I took this endeavor seriously.

As part of adjusting to a sober life, I printed and placed several pieces of paper around my house with the phrase: "I release the need for drugs and alcohol in my life," along with a smiley face. I felt that the more I saw this mantra around the house, the more motivated I'd be to say it aloud, and that might help attract the sober reality I was seeking.

It's been three and a half years since that fateful day.

Though Las Vegas was the grounds of my rock bottom, I refused to let that be my last memory of my time in Sin City. Instead, I chose to stay and rebuild my image.

At the time of this writing, I'm three and a half years sober and counting. How did I get here? Well, I found my purpose in life, and that purpose is to help people heal from their traumas. I can draw from my experiences and use them as a source of inspiration—not just for myself to remain sober, but for others as well.

Final Thoughts

This section is the perfect summation for all the stories in *Mayhem to Miracles*. Sometimes we don't know what we are made of until we start to fall apart, and our best parts pop out to hold us together. Our best part can be in the form of a daughter's love as in the case of Rev. Ariel. This section celebrates the resilience of authors who refused to give up while traveling that long and winding road we call life. Even hitting rock bottom did not stop them. They found their inner voice, connected with their inner selves, found the miracle in their monsters, and embraced hope for a better life. Their stories showed us how the worst things in life, like Jill Vanderwood's bullying and Sharla's and Mehdi's addictions, were the mayhem that created the miracles. When all else seemed to fail, some of the authors, like James Redfield, found that returning to nature and sleeping under the stars was the answer to continuing down a road full of pitfalls and miracles. For some of us, "hitting rock bottom" is the beginning of our miracle.

PART 5
WORDS OF WISDOM AND ENCOURAGEMENT
If I Knew Then What I Know Now

You are a beautiful soul
With a place in the universe,
A purpose to fulfill,
Wisdom to share.

If given the opportunity for deep reflection, would you have done anything differently in your life? Imagine being able to step into a time machine, travel back in life to meet yourself in your past, and share a few words of insight. Our authors have done just that for you, and we hope you enjoy their words of wisdom and encouragement.

Kathleen O'Keefe-Kanavos

If I knew then what I know now, I would have spent less time collecting "stuff," both emotional and physical, and spent more time focused on loved ones. Memories bring me more joy than boxes of physical stuff, and memories can be more easily retrieved from the closets of my mind.

Rev. Ariel Patricia

Rumi, a 13th century mystic, is quoted as saying *"The wound is the place where the Light enters you."* I believe we view the circumstances of our lives through our fears and insecurities, at times creating mayhem. Looking through the lens of our wounds also shows us opportunities where we can heal, grow, and expand, and gives us an opportunity for miracles. When you feel you're in the mayhem, ask yourself: "What if what I believe, may not be entirely true?"

Sister Dr. Jenna

There are three key teachings that I inculcate in myself and encourage others to do so. First, for us to learn about the self and to stay in a higher dimension, it is crucial to consider ourselves a soul. Second, we should make our relationship with God an intimate priority. When we have challenges and insecurities, it is because of past, unresolved issues—and when we can't be at peace with them, it's a sign of our disconnection to Source at that time. And thirdly, don't judge anyone. If you can live your life without judging anyone, and loving everybody the same, you experience inner peace and happiness.

Bernie Siegel, MD

The only thing I would change is myself, because of what I have learned about myself and life. I would not try to change other people. Let them be who they are and teach me about life. Experience is the greatest of teachers. What I call "natives" understand life, versus the "tourists" who are just passing through. For all my "children," remember, when things go wrong, God is redirecting you and something good will come of this. Life is a labor pain. Give birth to yourself and make the pain worthwhile. Flat tires can delay you, but spiritual flat tires might end up improving or even saving your life.

Laura Staley

A rich, deep, and anchored internal life filled with courage, hope, and belief in the very best of yourself and other people can fuel your strength and help see you to stable ground. The capacity to nurture unconditional love, compassion, and commitment to take the next right actions has been expanding for a lifetime. You chose this exceptional soul path to glean wisdom to contribute, love, and serve others. You do not ever have to doubt your value, your reason for being on this Earth, now or ever. You are loved. You matter.

Tamara Knox

To be different, perform differently, or live differently, one must be aware and have self-knowledge about their behaviors, beliefs, and reactions. If I were given the opportunity to have done something different in my life, I would have learned to address my fears and insecurities instead of letting them control my life. To live in fear is to minimize joy, to obstruct the joy we find. Simply stated, fear keeps us from our highest essence. If I would have known that my thoughts and beliefs were sabotaging me and keeping me from freedom, joy, and love, I would have made it a priority to discover another way of viewing my world.

Mehdi Bouneb

If I were to make a trip back in time to meet my former self, I would hug it, hold its hand, and let it know that the hardships we experienced were designed to help us evolve into the being we were destined to become. My dream of becoming a shaman is paved by the actions of my past, and because of this, I wouldn't tell my former self to change anything. As cliché as it sounds, everything happens for a reason. By working toward my dream, I get to be the shaman my past needs to heal. Healing is evolution.

Eileen Bild

Life has a way of showing us how to live so when we get to a point in the future, rather than hindsight, we can feel empowered by the choices we have made. Higher awareness, with the understanding that there is always a way, gives us the opportunity to live life to the fullest. There will be curve balls on our journey, but we can rise above them. We do not need to wait for those bumps in the road to learn the lessons. The principles of the universe are entwined in our Earthly endeavors. Watch, wait, listen, and then act.

Lori Walker

That my healing journey would be like The Yellow Brick Road in *The Wizard of Oz*. You never know who you will meet along the way! The lessons learned from each person I encountered, both good and bad, shaped my perceptions and my future. Mary opened my eyes to a new world of possibilities. But most importantly, she believed in me. She needed someone to pour her heart into, and I needed someone to help me rise above the mayhem. The perfect words, spoken at the perfect time to the perfect person, can change the course of someone's life forever.

Mary Ellen Lucas

The truth of the priest's words, "All is okay," heard that long-ago Christmas Day, brought a miraculous shift to my perspective. I've learned to be at peace with not knowing why my son Sean endured what he did. Much will remain a mystery. What I have come to believe is that there is something intangible within us all, an indwelling Light that is never sullied nor touched by illness. This inner wellspring exists even in the midst of suffering. It is a Light that consistently shines the "all is okay" message, no matter the challenge.

Sharla Charpentier

If I knew then that I was created perfectly and that, by following my heart, I would always stay on the right path, the peace and joy I had as a child would have continued and there would have been no mayhem. I would not have used alcohol as a coping mechanism. I would not have listened to others at the expense of myself. Now that I have the wisdom that only comes by way of dealing with the mayhem endured, I go to any lengths to preserve my sobriety, serenity, and spirituality. And my life is full of miracles.

Jill Ammon Vanderwood

If I had known then what I know now, I would not let fear overcome me and hold me back in life. I never knew that I had a voice and that others could benefit from my storytelling abilities. However, one can find their path or their life's calling at any age; it's never too late. I have learned so much during my time as a writer and speaker that, with God's help, I have a paved pathway into a bright future ahead. With every step comes another chance to change direction.

Karuna

Looking back, I don't think I'd change a thing. The life I have lived has gotten me to where I am today, which is harvesting the fruit of an awakened and engaged life and lifestyle. I've been privileged to live several lives: daughter and student, successful model and actress, wife and mother, entrepreneur, yogini, lifestyle and wellness coach, and even helicopter pilot! Each of those life stages led quite seamlessly to the next, and each one was filled with growing, maturing, and moving from fulfillment to fulfillment. That is the message and meaning of the Yogic life.

Bonnie McLean

Over my years in the healing professions, I have learned that we are all healers. Our bodies know how to heal themselves. They just need a boost and support sometimes. Love is the most important ingredient in the healing process. This may come from a professional healer or from family and friends. We also have to love ourselves enough to be able to receive that love from others and to give ourselves the attention and nurturing needed to shift our body and mind into its self-healing mode.

LE Gray

I am thrilled that I didn't know then what I know now. For if I had, I would not have tripped, stumbled, cracked, or crumbled. I might not have cried, screamed, or laughed until my belly ached. I might have kissed more and learned less. However, by looking in the rearview mirror, I might actually miss out on loving the imperfect person whom I see in the mirror today. Yes, pain comes from not knowing. However, I have earned my scars, which have now evolved into wings. For that, I am grateful.

Judy Lemon

Follow your heart...or your gut. The indigenous teachers I've worked with believe that we have three brains. There's the one in our heads, which they often refer to with uncomplimentary names, but we also have two others in our heart and abdominal areas. While we obviously need our head brains, our ego, logic, and doubt can often throw large rocks in our paths when important decisions have to be made. Much has been said about listening to your gut or following your heart, and there's a good reason for this: the information that comes through these "brains" is pure and true and will never lead you wrong. It's also a lot more subtle, so we must learn not only to listen, but to believe. When we can do this, we are truly in the flow.

Dr. Anne Worth

1 Corinthians 13:5—Love keeps no record of wrongs. I kept a long list. I couldn't forgive those who hurt me as a child, and despite any vows made at the wedding altar, I wouldn't continue to love someone who had betrayed me. My worst offense was my self-hatred. It was impossible for me to show grace or mercy to myself or others because I had no God to help me. It was only through His eyes, late in my life, that I understood we are all merely human beings—children needing the help of a Father.

Laura Rowley

Upon reflection, I would have corralled my wounded ego, not permitting self-recrimination. The phrase, "I should have known better" was a way to bury the pain of embarrassing mistakes. I laugh now, knowing we come to this lifetime to learn. We can't learn our lessons in advance of experiencing the highs and the lows. Carl Jung once said, "Life really does begin at forty. Up until then, you are just doing research." Life lessons need not be painful when seen through this positive lens.

Myriam Ben Salem

As counterintuitive as it may sound, if I knew then what I know now, I wouldn't have wished to change a single detail. I like to believe that the Universe knows better. No matter how harsh every event that took place in my life without my permission might have been, it was always exactly what I needed to unlearn my lifetime of conditioning, clear the dust, and get closer to my authentic self. It seems to me that when we start seeing every challenge as a blessing in disguise and face the pain courageously, our chaos naturally falls into place.

Rev. Sandra Kitt

I would make my own decisions about healthcare and learn about alternative forms of healing, such as energy, Chinese, and functional medicine. I'd eat healthy whole foods and focus on brain health nutrition, only using prescription medication as a last resort. More meditation and mindfulness would help me to stay centered and balanced, and I'd spend more time in nature connecting with Mother Earth. I would allow nothing outside myself to define my identity. And I'd listen to my heart, instead of my head, and not take things for granted or wait to follow my dreams.

Diane Vich

I would have learned to change my perspective and not take things personally. Allowing judgments and criticism from others to give my inner critic power over me only made the rollercoaster ride more painful. As I peeled away the layers of judgment and criticism that had impacted my health for more than twenty years, the physical symptoms unraveled. And as I focused on self-love and self-forgiveness, everything became easier. Through Orgazmik healing, I was able to maintain a sense of gratitude for life, empowering a consistent flow through life's obstacles by embracing them as opportunities.

Deborah Beauvais

What I know now that I didn't know many years ago, is this: Everything is presented to us so we may grow our souls and expand our consciousness. We are both soul and human while on Earth with an opportunity to learn from all our experiences, from the minute to the most challenging. It is our choice to learn, grow and prosper, or allow the experience to hinder a joy-filled life.

Jill Landry

Give and receive love freely. Know how important that is. Know you are worthy of that. Cherish those moments of just sitting with or talking with family members and friends, furry and human. Cherish the moments that feel insignificant. Those are the ones you may long to have back when they have passed. Take time to speak kind words. Be kind to yourself. Let go of being so hard on yourself; it will only keep you trapped where you are. Believe in the dreams that are in your heart. Believe in magic. Believe in yourself.

Peggy Willms

I would recognize my shortcomings as I walked through life and ask for help and guidance sooner. I agree with pushing the envelope and learning as you go—getting comfortable with being uncomfortable, as they say—but there comes a point when enough is enough. I wouldn't say it was ego that kept getting in the way, but perhaps in hindsight, it was. Especially as an entrepreneur, I learned quickly: If you do not want to fail or wind up exhausted and curled up in a corner, ask, ask, and then ask again. The power is in many. Build your tribe early!

Barbara A. Bertucci

I might have created a way to reframe my life lessons a bit sooner. I would have been gentler with myself. With these two skills, I would have owned "ME" sooner. I finally came to know that I am a child of God and that there are no mistakes. My mistakes created me. My uniqueness is what makes me special, compassionate, and loving. All my experiences are me, raw and yet defined. I am able to hear and see those who have walked similar paths and guide and comfort them. This is what my path and surrendering to my heart has taught me.

Teresa Velardi

If I knew then what I know now, I would spend more time with my loved ones. When I was younger, I would never have imagined what life would be like with those who were so dear to me living so far away. I grew up in a close-knit neighborhood, and as we moved away to our individual lives and new beginnings, the intention to "go back home" was there, but the ability to do so wasn't always. I would spend more time with people I love and forgive those who couldn't or wouldn't be there.

AFTERWORD

Hope is the Light in Our Dark
by Kathleen O'Keefe-Kanavos

*Hero's Journey stories have always been the way
essential lessons are taught and remembered.*

Being a part of this third book in the Sacred Stories series and working
with all the authors has been an immense privilege. Their stories have
changed my life. Many of the authors were returning "Sacred Story
Family Members." The series has created quite a fantastic family of
writers and friends.

There was such a strong need for a book such as this, a book that
highlighted the struggles many of us face daily and shared the positive
outcomes often orchestrated by Divine Intervention hidden in signs,
symbols, and synchronicities, as James Redfield so aptly wrote.

Mayhem bombards us in today's world, but we seldom hear about
the miracles that happen despite or because of the chaos. The miraculous
happy endings shared in each story were such a breath of fresh air, I
often read them multiple times. It is reassuring to see the good guy win
and ride off into the sunset on a white horse.

Hero's Journey stories have always been the way important lessons are taught and remembered. These journeys are unforgettable because the author refused to relent.

In high school, I sang in the school chorus. One of my favorite songs was the Richard Rodgers and Oscar Hammerstein II hit "You'll Never Walk Alone" which was later sung by many crooners, including Gerry and the Pacemakers and Elvis Presley. The lyrics that resonated with me most and exemplify this book are the ones that tell us to walk on! Don't stop... even if our dreams are tossed around because we will never walk alone.

So often, we feel alone in our times of need. We are sure no one else has experienced what we are feeling, so there is no hope for any help. Suddenly reading that someone else went through a similar life challenge and survived the devastation can help us continue one more day.

In a speech, Winston Churchill said, "If you're going through hell, keep going," and then discussed the "lion heart" of people. All of the authors in this book went through some form of hell, including me—but rather than giving up, they kept going. They embraced their lion hearts and followed the hope that led them forward on their Hero's Journey, until they came out the other side.

The dark hour of their soul became the fertile ground for their miracle. Without one, the other could not have existed.

My favorite part of the book is Part 5, where these incredible authors peered back into the dark from a place of light and shared their profound thoughts and insights with us. Their words of wisdom are worth their weight in gold.

Something else that was impressive to me in these stories was the belief in Divine Intervention, especially when a situation was at its worst. Divine faith combined with hope for a better day often made the difference between life and death.

When I think of hope, I think of the 1970s poster by Los Angeles photographer Victor Baldwin of a kitten clinging onto a bamboo pole with the words printed in bold letters beneath it, HANG IN THERE, BABY. Hope gives us reason to hang in there, for just one more day, hour, or minute. Hope is the light in our dark hour that guides us through the storms in life. Walk on....

May Miracles Abound
by Rev. Ariel Patricia

May you feel the peace and support of the angels and may miracles abound.

Forever hopeful,
Ariel

ADDITIONAL READING

Chaos to Clarity: Sacred Stories of Transformational Change – November 20, 2019, Sacred Stories Publishing, Kathleen O'Keefe-Kanavos (Co-Author), Rev. Patricia Cagganello (Co-Author), Bernie Siegel M.D. (Foreword), Deborah Beauvais, Eileen Bild, Tamara Knox, Teresa Velardi (Contributing Authors)

Crappy to Happy: Sacred Stories of Transformational Joy – October 6, 2020, Sacred Stories Publishing, Kathleen O'Keefe-Kanavos (Co-Author), Rev. Ariel Patricia (Co-Author), James Redfield (Foreword), Rev. Dr. Temple Hayes, Bernie Siegel M.D., Deborah Beauvais, Tamara Knox, Bonnie McLean OMD, Judy Lemon, Teresa Velardi, Diane Vich, Dr. Anne Worth (Contributing Authors)

Dreams That Can Save Your Life: Early Warning Signs of Cancer and Other Diseases – April 17, 2018, Findhorn/Inner Traditions, Larry Burk M.D. C.E.H.P. (Author), Kathleen O'Keefe-Kanavos (Author), Bernie Siegel M.D. (Foreword)

Surviving Cancerland: Intuitive Aspects of Healing – March 28, 2014 Cypress House, Kathleen O'Keefe-Kanavos (Author)

God is in the Little Things: Messages from the Animals – republished June 26, 2016, Sacred Stories Publishing, Patricia Brooks (Author)

God is in the Little Things: Messages from the Golden Angels – republished May 30, 2016, Sacred Stories Publishing, Patricia Brooks (Author)

Scanning for Signal – November 17, 2016, Sacred Stories Publishing, Patricia Brooks (Co-Author)

The Celestine Prophecy – September 18, 2018 (Reissue edition), Grand Central Publishing, James Redfield (Author)

The Tenth Insight: Holding the Vision – December 1, 1998, Grand Central Publishing, James Redfield (Author)

The Secret of Shambhala: In Search of the Eleventh Insight – November 1, 2001, Warner Books, James Redfield (Author)

The Twelfth Insight: The Hour of Decision – February 9, 2012, Grand Central Publishing, James Redfield (Author)

The Right to Be You – 2008, Temple Press, Temple Hayes (Author)

How to Speak Unity – 2010, DeVorss Publishing, Temple Hayes (Author)

When Did You Die? 8 Steps to Stop Dying Every Day and Start Waking Up – 2014, First Edition-HCI Publishing, Second Edition, Amazon Publishing, Temple Hayes (Author)

Love, Medicine & Miracles – 1998, Harper Perennial, Bernie Siegel, MD (Author)

Three Men Six Lives – 2020, Sacred Stories Publishing, Bernie Siegel, MD (Author)

When You Realize How Perfect Everything Is: A Conversation Between Grandfather and Grandson – 2020, Sacred Stories Publishing, Bernie Siegel, MD (Co-Author)

Highest Love: In Sacred Unity with Autoimmunity – June 2020, Tamara Knox (Author)

The Truth about IBS and Anxiety: Erasing the Symptoms Effortlessly – January 14, 2020, Diane M. Vich (Author)

Goddess Diaries: A Walk in the Tuscan Sun – March 27, 2019, Veronica Roze (Author)

Integrative Medicine: The Return of the Soul to Healthcare – 2015; Balboa Press, Bonnie McLean OMD (Author)

Live Inspired – April 2020, Sacred Stories Publishing, Laura Staley (Author)

Let Go Courageously and Live with Love: Transform Your Life with Feng Shui – July 2016, Laura Staley (Author)

Cherish Your World Gift Book of 100 Tips to Enhance Your Home and Life – Sept. 2018, Laura Staley (Author)

Call me Worthy: Unlocking a Painful Past for a Glorious Future – 2019, Dr. Anne Worth (Author)

The Paper Doll Kids – December 2019, Deborah Beauvais (Author)

The Rebirth of a Soul: Life Insights from a Simple Dude – November 17, 2017, Page Publishing, Mehdi Bouneb (Author)

The Day the Goose Squabble Stopped – 2019, Sacred Stories Publishing, Mary Ellen Lucas (Author)

The Goslings Learn to Listen – 2020, Sacred Stories Publishing, Mary Ellen Lucas (Author)

Goodbye to Grandpa Geezer Goose – 2021, Sacred Stories Publishing, Mary Ellen Lucas (Author)

The Llove Llama Travels the 7 Continents – December 10, 2020, Authentic Endeavors Publishing, Sharla Charpentier (Co-Author)

Ned the Narwhal Voyages the 5 Oceans – 2021, Authentic Endeavors Publishing, Sharla Charpentier (Co-Author)

Drugs Make You Un-Smarter – February 1, 2011, Jill Ammon Vanderwood (Co-Author)

Shaking Behind the Microphone: Overcoming the Fear of Public Speaking – Nov. 6, 2013, Jill Ammon Vanderwood (Author)

Erase the Problem of Bullying – August 24, 2015, All Things that Matter Press, Jill Ammon Vanderwood (Author)

Off Target: The Path You Choose #1 – February 2, 2019, Idea Creations Press, Jill Ammon Vanderwood (Author)

1 Habit to Beat Cancer: Secrets of the Happiest Cancer Thrivers on the Planet – April 12, 2020, Barbara A. Bertucci (Contributing Author)

BOOK CLUB QUESTIONS

1. Which story in the book *Mayhem to Miracles* affected you the most and why?

2. As Laura Staley so aptly phrased, "Two lives like two pearls formed from all the grit inside the oyster." How does the grit in our lives create pearls of wisdom?

3. Dr. Bernie Siegel weaves the story of flat tires in his life as history repeating itself to impart an important message. How has this concept of repeated history played out in your life and world conflict?

4. Was there ever mayhem in your life that became a miracle? How did hope impact the outcome?

5. Do you believe a miracle can take place without mayhem preceding it?

MEET OUR CONTRIBUTORS

Rev. Dr. Temple Hayes is an author, spiritual leader, and difference-maker. She is the CEO of First Unity Spiritual Campus, which transcends religious denominations, embraces all ethnicity, and reaches beyond national borders. She is also on the leadership team of the Association of Global New Thought and is the founder of illli.org, an online university for lifelong learners and people called to be difference-makers through powerful leadership. templehayes.com

Deborah J. Beauvais is an intuitive, energy practitioner, author and founder of global Dreamvisions 7 Radio Network and Kids 4 Love Project all fostering love, unity, and elevated consciousness. dreamvisions7radio.com

Myriam Ben Salem is a suicide survivor, a lifelong learner, an edutainer, an unapologetic truth-teller, a stoic philosophy lover. Deeply passionate about everything life has to offer, she is frequently described as vivacious, compassionate, authentic, warrior, bold, and always seeking the best way forward for herself and every person she interacts with.

Barbara A. Bertucci is an intuitive healer, wellness consultant, and an animal, life rights advocate. https://www.foreveryoungsolutions.com

Eileen Bild is CEO of Ordinary to Extraordinary Life, OTEL Productions, OTEL Universe. Along with her husband, they have a world-renowned multi-media and production company specializing in ROKU Channel Development for individuals, businesses and non-profits and video productions. Eileen is also a columnist, published author, and Breakthrough S.P.A.R.K. Coach. www.corethinkingblueprint.com

Mehdi Bouneb is a thirty-year-old citizen of the world. Today, he pursues his dream of becoming a shaman while continuing his Master's in Counseling Psychology. His purpose is to open a healing home centered around shamanism and addiction counseling to help people from all walks of life heal from their traumas.

Sharla Charpentier is a mother of four, lawyer, writer, and artist. She co-authored *The Llove Llama Travels the 7 Continents* and *Ned the Narwhal Voyages the 5 Oceans*, the first books in The Llove Llama and Friends series. She brought to life The Llove Llama and Friends characters through her drawings. thellovellamaandfriends.com

LE Gray is the founder of IPride, a successful youth empowerment program, and co-founder of IPride Life Coaching. A published author, living kidney donor and a fervent advocate for sexual assault victims, LE is a proud mother of 3 sons and 3 dogs. Visit ipride.net and ipridelifecoaching.com.

Sister Dr. Jenna is the director of the Brahma Kumaris Meditation Museums and host of the America Meditating Radio Show. She serves as an Evolutionary Leader and was selected by Empower a Billion Women 2020 as one of 100 Most Influential Leaders of 2015. She is also a recipient of the President's Lifetime National Community Service

Award and a trusted spiritual mentor committed to bridging divides in societies. americameditating.org

Karuna is a celebrated Yogini, founder of lightonkundalini.com, co-founder of Light on Light Publications & Press and a Yoga spokesperson on VoiceAmerica and other media. Karuna works to bring the values and vision of Yogic lifestyle to people everywhere.

Rev. Sandra Kitt is a retired Major in the United States Army, author, and coach. Currently she is part of the First Unity Ministry team in St. Petersburg, Florida and is committed to helping people thrive at thrivingheartsministry.com, revsandrakitt.com.

Tamara Knox M.Msc, Ph.D is an International bestselling author of the book *In Sacred Unity with Autoimmunity*. She has co-authored a number of books relating to the metaphysical, self-love, and healing. She believes the foundation to wholeness can be attained through self-awareness, sound, breath, food and movement. She encourages self-exploration on all levels. shekhinahpath.com

Jill Landry loves both science and creative pursuits. Jill has studied holistic health modalities, culinary arts, aerial arts, and movement sciences. She enjoys sharing with others through teaching and writing.

Judy Lemon is a shamanic practitioner of the Rio Napo lineage in Peru. She is also a certified trauma therapist with a private practice in Southern California. She brings her extensive experience and knowledge into her work of helping others to develop their own spiritual gifts. judylemon. com

Mary Ellen Lucas is an Interfaith / Interspiritual minister, author of the children's books series Life on Little Puddle Pond, and a spiritual mentor and ceremony officiant. www.thelovingway.me.

Bonnie McLean O.M.D., A.P. is a Doctor of Oriental Medicine and Acupuncture Physician licensed in the State of Florida. She received her B.S. in Nursing from Duke University and her MA in Counseling from Pepperdine University. She has practiced in the fields of medicine and healing for 57 years. Bonnie is a lecturer and author of *Integrative Medicine.* spiritgatemedicine.com

James Redfield is the author of *The Celestine Prophecy* series of books, writer/producer of the Celestine Prophecy Movie, and co-founder of celestinevision.com, where he is active with the CP Community, and Celestine Coaching. celestinevision.com

Laura Rowley is an international animal communicator who holds private sessions addressing clients' questions to pets. Her podcast, Animal Connections with Laura Rowley on Dreamvisions7RadioNetwork, explores the profound revelations of our shared lives with beloved pets. laurarowleyhealer.com

Bernie Siegel, MD is a NY Times bestselling author, lecturer, founder of ECaP (Exceptional Cancer Patients) and a retired pediatric/general surgeon. Bernie has been called a leading teacher of the Mind-Body Connection and is well known for his groundbreaking book *Love, Medicine and Miracles*. Bernie is also the author of *Three Men Six Lives* his first novel and co-author with his grandson Charlie Siegel of their book of short writings and poetry *When You Realize How Perfect Everything Is.* berniesiegelmd.com

Laura Staley is the founder of Cherish Your World. Laura passionately supports people by guiding them to holistic transformations of space, heart, and life. Laura writes personal essays focused on self-discovery, feng shui, and emotional health. She's the author of *Live Inspired, Let Go Courageously,* and *Cherish Your World Gift Book.* cherishyourworld.com

Jill Ammon Vanderwood is an author and speaker from Idaho, with eleven published books. Her most recent book, *Off Target* is the winner of the Mom's Choice Award. www.jillvanderwood.com

Teresa Velardi is an author, speaker, publisher, and potter. Committed to making a difference in the lives of others, she uses her gifts to help people get their stories told in books. Teresa is currently publishing children's and international books. bookendeavors.com

Diane Vich is a multi-talented registered nurse and health coach. She helps people overcome chronic illness and pain through a mind, body and soul connection by treating the individual as a holistic and multifaceted person. Diane helps clients overcome chronic disease, and negative patterns that impact their health by using Orgazmik healing. dianevich.com

Lori Walker is a Usui Reiki Master Practitioner, Holy Fire Reiki Master, a founding member of Book Club-Pittsburgh, and featured on the cover of the 2021 Women's Yellow Pages of Greater Pittsburgh. Two of her poems, Tomorrow and I Want To Know were published in Women's Independent Press.

Peggy Willms has been a trend setter for 30+ years as a personal trainer, nutritionist, health/wellness and life coach, manager of multi-million dollar medical clinics, corporate wellness programs, cutting-edge radio host, and executive producer and coach for her live coaching docuseries. She is a mom of two men and a grandma. peggywillms.com

Dr. Anne Worth is a Christian counselor, author, and speaker. She serves homeless people, abused animals, and Sudanese refugees in her community. Sharing her testimony and helping others find their life purpose is her greatest joy. Her hobby is creating crosses and other Christian art using vintage jewelry. dranneworthauthor.com

MEET OUR AUTHORS

Rev. Ariel Patricia felt the calling to found Sacred Stories Publishing and Media after a series of events changed the course of her life. Since then, she has been on a heart-based mission to help others tell and share their own stories of transformation to a global audience.

Promptly after this period in her life, Ariel left her career in the corporate and educational worlds and entered One Spirit Interfaith Seminary in New York, where she became ordained as an interfaith minister. This deepened her passion to share the profound experiences and wisdom of Spirit to those who are ripe to receive it.

Now, as both sacred storyteller and visionary businesswoman, Ariel is the powerhouse behind Sacred Stories Publishing and Media. Her leadership in the rapidly evolving fields of publishing, broadcasting, and online learning has quickly put SSPM on the map as a conscious business enterprise with a soul for helping humanity prosper and expand our spiritual awareness.

As an ordained interfaith, interspiritual minister, Ariel Patricia believes every story is a sacred story. She is ordained from One Spirit Interfaith Seminary in New York and has earned her Master of Arts in

Education and her Bachelor of Science in Business. Ariel Patricia worked in the corporate and educational worlds for many years and proudly served six years as a sergeant in the U.S. Marine Corps.

Ariel Patricia is the author of two books sharing the beginning of her spiritual journey— *God is in the Little Things: Messages from the Animals* and *God is in the Little Things: Messages from the Golden Angels.* She is co-author of a poetry book, *Scanning For Signal,* and co-author of the first two books of the Sacred Stories of Transformation series: *Chaos to Clarity: Sacred Stories of Transformational Change* and *Crappy to Happy: Sacred Stories of Transformational Joy.*

Learn more at
https://sacredstories.com

Kathleen (Kat) O'Keefe-Kanavos is accredited in Psychopathology and Special Education. Kat taught Psychology at USF, Ft. Myers Branch, and taught the severely emotionally handicapped for ten years. She served as Special Education Department Head for two years before retiring.

Kat is also known as The Queen of Dreams in her internationally syndicated columns, *PR Guru*, and video podcaster/radio show host on DreamVisions7 Radio Network, *Dreaming Healing*. Kat is a three-time breast cancer survivor whose dreams diagnosed her illness, which was missed by the medical community and the tests on which they relied. Kat says, "My dreams and my doctors saved my life." She is also a multi-award-winning author and Dream Expert who has been seen on Dr. Oz, Doctors, NBC, and CBS. Kat and Duke University Radiologist Dr. Larry Burk co-wrote the 2018 Nautilus Award Winner, *Dreams That Can Save Your Life*. She is currently working on a co-authored series with Rev. Ariel Patricia of Sacred Stories Publishing. As a content editor, Kat helps authors with the organizing and writing of their books.

Kat's an international author/lecturer and keynote speaker who promotes patient advocacy and connecting with Divine-guidance through Dreams for success in health, wealth, and relationships. "Don't tell God how big your problems are. Tell your problems how big your God is."

Learn more at kathleenokeefekanavos.com

ENDNOTES

The Psychology of Hope

1. Elpis, Greek Mythology.com https://www.greekmythology.com/Other_Gods/Minor_Gods/Elpis/elpis.html
2. *The Anatomy of Hope: How People Prevail in the Face of Illness*, by Jerome Groopman; Random House Trade Paperbacks; Reprint edition (January 11, 2005) The Anatomy of Hope Quotes by Jerome Groopman. https://www.goodreads.com/work/quotes/252742-the-anatomy-of-hope-how-people-prevail-in-the-face-of-illness

CPSIA information can be obtained
at www.ICGtesting.com
Printed in the USA
LVHW021034270921
698794LV00001B/8